LORD! "WHY ME?"

Joanna D. Price

© Copyright 2006 Joanna D. Price
All rights reserved. No part of this publication may be reproduced, stored in a retrieval system, or transmitted, in any form or by any means, electronic, mechanical, photocopying, recording, or otherwise, without the written prior permission of the author.

Scripture taken from the HOLY BIBLE: NEW INTERNATIONAL VERSION®. NIV® Copyright © 1973, 1978, 1984 by International Bible Society. Used by permission of The Zondervan Corporation.

The "NIV" and "New International Version" trademarks are registered in the United States Patent and Trademark Office by International Bible Society.

Note for Librarians: A cataloguing record for this book is available from Library and Archives Canada at www.collectionscanada.ca/amicus/index-e.html
ISBN 1-4120-7045-7

Offices in Canada, USA, Ireland and UK
This book was published on-demand in cooperation with Trafford Publishing. On-demand publishing is a unique process and service of making a book available for retail sale to the public taking advantage of on-demand manufacturing and Internet marketing. On-demand publishing includes promotions, retail sales, manufacturing, order fulfilment, accounting and collecting royalties on behalf of the author.

Book sales for North America and international:
Trafford Publishing, 6E–2333 Government St.,
Victoria, BC V8T 4P4 CANADA
phone 250 383 6864 (toll-free 1 888 232 4444)
fax 250 383 6804; email to orders@trafford.com
Book sales in Europe:
Trafford Publishing (UK) Limited, 9 Park End Street, 2nd Floor
Oxford, UK OX1 1HH UNITED KINGDOM
phone 44 (0)1865 722 113 (local rate 0845 230 9601)
facsimile 44 (0)1865 722 868; info.uk@trafford.com
Order online at:
trafford.com/05-1956
10 9 8 7 6 5 4 3 2

DEDICATION

I dedicate this book in loving memory of my daughter, Lakesia L, Davis-Gilbert. During my life, it was her death that brought greater understanding of the will of God. In her leaving, I found clarity and understanding to the meaning of having a "Job experience."

In addition, this book has been dedicated to those individuals who have suffered by the hands of people whom they trusted. It has been written especially for those that have endured unnecessary heartaches, pain and disappointments believing they had no avenue of escape.

In an effort to encourage and inspire individuals of all walks of life who discover themselves entangled in life's challenges, I have allowed the Holy Spirit to direct me as I tell my story of how I overcame and receive victory through my adversities.

I especially would like to thank each and every one that caused me to cry, abused me, disappointed me and inflicted unnecessary pain into my life. You played a significant role in pushing me into my destiny. Without you, I would have never attempted to write nor publish this book.

CONTENTS

Poem 6
Foreword 7
Acknowledgements 9
Preface 11
Introduction 14
Lord! Why Me? 19
A Kiss Of Betrayal 27
Judas Iscariot, Son Of Satan 29
Trouble Is In This House 33
Trouble Is In Job's Home 38
A Wounded Heart 42
A Broken Heart 54
A Deceitful Heart 66
A Shattered Heart 88
Weeping May Endure For A Night 121
The Death Of Lazarus 127
Count It All Joy 129
God Is A Deliverer 135
Moses, Chosen Deliverer Of The Israelites 140
Barak And Deborah 146
Epilogue 148
Bibliography 149
About The Author 150

LORD! "WHY ME?"

Lord, Why Me? Though you have chosen me;
I am willing to go through the trials of life.
As I travel through this foreign land
I know that I can hold your hand.
For I maybe weak in flesh and bones;
Yet in your strength I can hold on.
There will come a day when this world
Will fade.
This, I know, and is the reason why I got saved.
So Lord, give me spiritual wisdom, so that
Faith may grow.
And if I forget and do not know, in your
Arms I shall go.
So when I'm faced with trials of life;
I look to You for Your advise.
Life will have it's up's and downs;
But Jesus, my Lord and Savior will always
Be around.
In His arms, I am bound.
Now Lord, when I'm surrounded by the
Troubles of life. In Your word, Lord, will I suffice.

Author: Teneshia Bailey

FOREWORD

I can still feel the heat of the sun on my face and the smell of the dirt as we picked tomatoes for a days wage. I recall my Mother saying, "Baby time will bring about a change for the good and for the bad, for all of us if we keep on living." This is exactly what time has done for my friend and cousin Dr. Price, affectionately known as Bonnie.

It seems as though it was just yesterday that we sat around the comfort of our little living room discussing our individual hopes and dreams, never imaging the trials we would encounter.

Yet, one day God called her out and this time she answered His call. Bonnie gave God her whole heart, soul and spirit just to do His will.

The trials came-the heat was intensified and there was a time in Bonnie life when she would have asked "Lord! Why me?" But in the midst of the burning fiery furnace, He, God's Holy Spirit would whisper in her ear, "Stand still and see the salvation of the Lord; for you are not alone, I am with you."

Bonnie has learned to trust and obey God's Word. She has allowed His Word to become a light unto her path. Even when the storms of life were raging and her life appeared as though it would be tossed to and fro as a battered ship. She never allowed the illusions of the enemy to cause her to waiver or to give in to his tricks.

I say to Bonnie, Dr. Price; there will be other storms and many more battles to fight. As I see you in the spiritual realm, you are dressed for battle, and you shout out your battle cry. "For God is on my side: who shall then stand against Him."

I see you looking towards the heavens: you are in awe of this awesome God. You are singing a love song to Him. "I worship you oh God of heavens and earth, may you reign forever." Why not me Lord, why not me, for your sake alone, why not me?

I say to you Dr. Price, you have beaten the odds that were against you. You have become the beautiful butterfly that God intended you to be. Soar. Soar high! Allow His breath to direct your wings. He will take you places, you only dreamed of those hot summer days on that tomato field. I love you, cousin, and I will always be here.

Darcel L. Clemens

ACKNOWLEDGEMENTS

To my children, Willie, Shannetta, Reginald, Renard Jr and Ryan, I love you all.

To my twenty seven grandchildren, especially Patrice and Paulkeria Ingram, Jeffery Tyree Roberts, Shamiah S, Kennedy, Trinity and Isaiah Reginald Davis.

To Teneshia C. Bailey, my oldest granddaughter who wrote the poem, "Lord! Why Me?"

To Teria S. Davis-Bailey, my second grandchild, for the beautiful cover illustration and for editing the final edition of Lord, Why Me."

To Stacy Carla Gilbert, for the improvement you made in all aspects of your life, especially after the passing of your Mother and while I completed this book.

To my dear friends: Patrice Gilbert and Juannetta Jones who edited my work and encouraged me when it appeared I had giving up.

To my sister, Robin M. Prince: for supporting me mentally, emotionally and financially. What would I have done if I did not have a sister like her?

To my God-daughter, Carrilee N. Brown, (Shug) who eagerly listened as I read segments of this book to her.

To my aunt and Pastor, Katherine Dames who listened to me as I cried over challenges that I faced. For the prayers she prayed and the spiritual advice she imparted in me when I believed I could no longer go on.

To my sister-in-law, Amanda L. Ford, who supported me during the death of my daughter, Kesia. For all the encouraging words and for just lending a helping hand wherever needed.

To my baby sister: Kimberly Ash who tried to edit the final penmanship of my book.

Photo by Sears Portrait Studio: the Florida Mall; Orlando, Florida.

Book covering vision by Renee Bethea: my cousin.

And finally, to a very special friend: Renard Price, Sr. for the support, for your friendship, for the many calls and for being there regardless of our differences.

PREFACE

Have you ever wondered how some people seem to skip through life with little or no bruises, life for them appears to be a bed of roses. They seem to have it all, while others struggle with issues of life.

Some people live as though there will be no tomorrow, while others cling to life realizing that it is a precious commodity.

Life is a mystery, full of surprises. At times, it may appear that life has come in a box wrapped with a big red ribbon. And at other times, life might hit you like a giant tidal wave crushing heavenly upon you, throwing you fiercely against the sea of life. It is like a merry go round, going up and down, round and around.

However, it is what you make of it and will consist of many trials and tribulations. Challenges and changes come to make you strong, to break you down and push you into your destiny. For these things enhances one's ability to grow and develop as an individual.

Life is a gift from God and should not be taken for granted. It is something that must be managed. A person can choose to be happy, or they can decide to sit around and be sad: concentrating on negative things of their past.

Nevertheless, the question that this person should ask themself is what will I gain from allowing this portion of my life to feaster? Will it breed bitterness, envy, jealousy, hatred and strife among others? Is it worth harboring? Or should it be discarded from my life entirely?

A life of happiness consists of making sound decisions. Decisions which evolve around healthy choices, and plans that include God in all of our dealings.

Understanding the "Cycle of Life," as according to Ecclesiastes 3:1-8 is an essential part of understanding life changes. This scripture allows an individual to realize mishaps are going to crop up in life and they will go away. The "Cycle of Life" helps us to understand that there will be situations and circumstances of life that we may or may not could have avoided.

The Book of Ecclesiastes, Chapter 3 is a scripture of actuality, providing an individual with the realization that life will have many ups and downs. Seasons will come and they will go. Ecclesiastes 3:1-8 declares (italics):

To everything there is a time and a season, and a time to every purpose under the heavens.
A time to be born, and a time to die; A time to plant, and a time to pluck up that which is planted; A time to kill, and a time to heal; a time break down, and a time to build up;
A time to weep, and a time to laugh; a time to mourn, and a time to dance;
A time to cast away stones, and a time to gather stones together; a time to embrace, and a time to refrain from embracing;
A time to get, and a time to lose; a time to keep; and a time to cast away; A time to rend, and a time to sew; a time to keep silence, and a time to speak;
A time to love, and a time to hate, a time of war and a time of peace.

In other words, there will be seasons in which an individual will experience change. Many of these changes will come without warning and others may come as a welcome release to some uneventful episode of life. Changes such as, death is inevitable.

Regardless of the season, why not learn from each of them? Grow in joy, face each challenge and appreciate the times of laughter. Learn from those seasons which are difficult, while remembering that trouble does not last always and has come only for a season.

Life in and of itself can be joyous, bringing with it much happiness or it can be complicated, bringing a tremendous amount of heartaches. So severe until it makes a person regret being born. Pain which can be felt deep within that causes an individual to say unto God, "Lord! Why Me?"

Someone may ask, "Lord! Why Me? Why so much pain? Why so much heartaches? Why so many tears? Why so much rain? When will the sun shine again, are better days ahead? "God on the other hand, might respond by saying: "My child, why not you? For I have made thee and it is I, who am aware of how much you can bear."

INTRODUCTION

Are you a person who goes through life experiencing one hardship after another? Each time you get over a hurdle it appears another is awaiting you. As a matter of fact, challenges and trials are all you know. To alleviate the pain you find release through drugs, sex, medication, alcohol, isolation and denial of the problem. However, there are times when life burdens appear too heavy to bear and you cry out, Lord! Why Me?

Have you ever watched a woman as she prepares for motherhood? She begins to glow as she feels her baby growing within. As this fetus starts to grow and develop within her womb, her emotion shifts into overdrive. For nine months she pampers herself, prides herself in knowing she is about to bring a child into this world.

When this baby is born, this mother does everything in her power to protect this child. She watches over it as though she was a mother lion. As this child journey through life, she may become overly protective not allowing or wanting the child to venture to far from her. For this mother knows that the road that he/she travels will not come without mishaps.

Then there are those Mom's who could care less about her unborn child. For some unknown reason, she cannot develop an emotional bond with this infant. She may have conceived this baby through casual sex, therefore not having a real connection with the child's father. When this happens, there is usually no commitment from either party (the father nor the mother) the child suffers and the couple regrets ever meeting each other.

This child goes through life feeling the affects of its parent inability to be responsible. They fumble in life wondering why life has been so harsh for them and oftentimes history repeats itself.

The birth of a child should be a joyous occasion, but it does come with a price. There are financial obligations, sometimes unforeseen health problems, child care, after care, nurturing and just caring for the child can be a burden. For some parents these things may be a bit strenuous.

The birth of a child can bring with it love, hate, separation, divorce, and even the death of a relationship. This is exactly what happened to my parents while I was in my mother's womb.

"Lord! Why Me?" has been written as a result of the things that happened to this author throughout life. It has been written to provide spiritual guidance to those individuals who have found themselves in situations un-liken to God's commands.

It is based on actual events of this author's life. Her hope is to provide the reader with an understanding of how to overcome obstacles using the Word of God as a source of reference.

It has not been written with the aim of insulting nor to embarrass the reader or anyone that may read its contents.

However, its main purpose is to inspire, enlighten, and to enrich the spiritually deprived as well as the individual who may have been or who is caught in an unstable relationship.

This book was written with the hope of changing minds and attitudes. Chapters were written under the directions of the Holy Spirit with the end result bringing healing to the wounded in heart, and restoration to the broken in spirit.

Certain chapters will reveal the many spiritual battles that this author encountered as a youngster, teenager, young adult and even as a married woman.

Throughout this book, one will find scriptures as a point of reference as to what God can and will do if we allow him to have His way in our life.

There will be chapters that also depict Satan's cunning tricks that interfere with God's plans for those He has chosen.

Life for this author has not been easy, however her relationship with God has brought much comfort and gratitude in knowing

God is true to His Word. It was this intimacy that has sustained her. She has come to realize that Christians must not lean to their own understanding and God must be acknowledged in everything we do.

This author has come to the conclusion that God will not place more on you than you can bear. He will see you through a test. He will require things of you, in an effort to test your faithfulness. As a representative of the cross, there will be numerous blows of life. Many of these afflictions will consisted of being talked about, persecuted, scorned, mocked and buked. However, they are just a test of your faithfulness to God. Like the people of the Bible, once the test has been passed, "He is a rewarder of them that diligently seek Him" (Heb 11:6, NIV).

It is equally important for every child of God to discern that as we travel through this life, Satan is standing ready with his demonic host throwing fiery darts our way. Henceforth, you should take the Sword of the Spirit and use it to defend yourself against the warfare of Satan.

Satan's ultimate goal is to "steal, kill, and destroy" as many of God's children as he can. In doing so, he will use every trick in the book. He will use your mind, body, heart and take your soul, if you let him. Therefore, when you are challenged with the worries of life and when it seems as though you have been placed in the burning furnace, given over to the lions for a meal, and called before the king, hold fast to your faith and say, "Lord, Why not me?"

Practicing Christians must comprehend that Satan is on his "JOB." Never taking a vacation, never getting sick and is recruiting as many souls as he can. His ultimate goal is to detour man from the will of God in any way he sees fit, with the anticipation of conquering his soul, causing man to receive eternal damnation as his final place of rest.

Satan will use daddy, mama, sister, brother, husbands, wives, girlfriends, boyfriends, and anyone he can submit his evil spirit upon. He disguises himself, coming in many forms, size and shapes. He is not recognized by many people until it is too late, tricking the saints of God as well.

He creates turmoil and worry in the mind of individuals desiring to serve God with all their heart. Inflicting pain and suffering upon those people that have made up their mind to walk aright before the Lord. Nevertheless, one must hold on to his faith, be steadfast and understand that the challenges of life assist in building character. They are as a testimony for those individuals who may be watching you to see how well you weather the storm. The Bible declares in I Peter 4:12: (NIV).

"Think it not strange concerning the fiery trial which is to try you, as though some strange thing happened unto you."
"But rejoice, inasmuch as ye are partakers of Christ's sufferings; that when his glory shall be revealed, ye may be glad also exceeding joy."

1

LORD! WHY ME?

Throughout our lives, we have heard over and over again that "man should not question God." Perhaps this may be true, especially if the question is presented in a derogative manner.

As it stand from a Biblical perspective, there is no written evidence that states, "man should not question God." This is clearly an assumption on man's part in reflecting his respect to an inerrant and infallible God.

Who would dare question a God who has the power to create the universe just by speaking it into existent? Who would pose a question to a God that has the power to make His very Words become flesh?

What man in his right mind would go before the almighty God and question how and why He created man in His own image and in His likeness? Why would any man believe he has the right to approach a God who has the ability to speak life or death upon him in a wink of an eye?

Most people who do not have an intimate relationship with God believe that they are not entitled to ask Him questions. Yet, when they find themselves in difficult situations they cry out "Lord, why me?

God in His infinite wisdom recognized the need for man to communicate, and because of this need, He created man after his own kind so that he would not be alone. However, His intent was for man to have relationship and to have fellowship with Him.

Therefore, it is important for man to know when it is appropriate for him to ask questions of God.

God gave of himself in the form of love. This token of love was a gift so that man could bond with Him. This kinship was not intended to be a one sided relationship. God's desire is for man to praise Him, pray to Him and most of all to talk with Him on a regular basis. This association alone would foster an environment that would spark curiosity in man allowing him to pose questions to God.

The Bible declares that we can ask whatsoever we will and we will receive a response from the Master. Therefore, it is through Him, and from Him that man can expect an answer.

Man must understand with out a doubt that all respect, honor, praise, thanks and glory belongs to God and He alone. For as long as man has lived, there has never been and never will be anyone as infallible as Him.

In life man will find himself questioning God, especially during difficult times. This is apart of man's nature. As people we are curious and we are constantly seeking understanding to those things we do not comprehend.

Man's relationship with God and His Son allows him to seek help in times of need. His relationship with God is very similar to that of a nature father. As it is in the flesh, so is it in the Spiritual realm. God's children can bring all of their needs and concerns to Him. This includes asking questions with respect to who God is.

It is because of this rapport that we are granted certain rights in seeking guidance and in asking whatsoever we have need of in the name of Jesus. Jesus died on the cross that we might have a right to go to the Father boldly. We can ask anything in Jesus' name and we shall receive it. Righteousness in heart provides us access to the kingdom.

Throughout the Bible there were numerous individuals who

asked questions of God. In many instances, those chosen by God for a particular task asked questions when they where unsure.

In searching the Bible, we can not find where God said unto man, thou shall not ask questions of me. In an effort to help man understand His expectations, He established rules and regulations in which man should adhere to.

These rules and regulations are known as the "Ten Commandments." They are the blueprint for man's life. If obeyed, man could avoid many snares and tangles of this world. The commandments have been famous for man's inability to abide by God's rule. Both man and woman ask the question, "Why would you (God) give us bodily sensations, if he did not desire us to fulfill our sexual appetite; then impose such a rule as "Thou shall not commit fornication/adultery upon us.

In the Book of Genesis, Cain was the first person to questioned God. He appeared arrogant, rude and rebellious of nature. Out of anger, He killed Abel, his brother. Abel offered up to God a more acceptable offering. God said unto Cain. "Where is Abel thy brother?" Cain responded by saying, "I know not: am I my brother's keeper?" (Gen 4:9, NIV).

God who is longsuffering and ever so merciful: allowed Cain to respond to Him in that manner. There is no place in the scripture where we find God reprimanding Cain: for his rude behavior. However, he is punished for the slaying of Abel, his brother. Instead, God responded by saying:

"What hast thou done? The voice of thy brother's blood crieth unto me from the ground" (vv 10, NIV).
And now art thou cursed from the earth, which hath opened her mouth to receive thy brother's blood from thy hand; when thou tillest the

> *ground it shall not hencefort yield,*
> *unto thee her strength; a fugitive*
> *and a vagabond shalt thou be in the*
> *earth" (vv 11, 12, NIV).*

Abram received word from God in a vision concerning his fate. In this vision, God made a covenant with him and promised to greatly reward him. However, Abram wanted to know what God was going to give him for his obedience and faithfulness. He asked:

> *"Lord God, what wilt thou give*
> *me, seeing I go childless, and the*
> *steward of my house is this Eliezer*
> *Damascus?" (Gen 15:1 & 2, NIV,*
> *italic added).*

God's answered by saying, **"Look now toward heaven, and tell the stars, if thou be able to number them: and he said unto him, So shall thy seed be"** *(vv 5: NIV).*

God reassured Abram of His plan for his life. He did not respond by saying, "Why are you questioning me, I am the Lord God, just look toward heaven."

However, God deals with Abram when He changes his name to Abraham. God promised to **"Make him a father of many nations, to make him exceedingly fruitful, and to make nations of him and kings shall come out of thee, saith the Lord God"** *(vv 5 & 6, NIV).*

"God said unto Abraham, As for Sarai thy wife, thou shalt not call her name Sarai, but Sarah shall her name be" (Genesis 17: 15, NIV).

After changing both their names, God began to restructure their lives. In doing so, *"He said unto Abraham, "I will bless her, (Sarah) and give thee a son also of her: and she shall be a mother of nations; kings of people shall be of her"* (Genesis 17:6, NIV).

Abraham's first reaction was to laugh, saying; "Shall a child be born unto him that is an hundred years old? Shall Sarah, that is ninety years old, bear?" (vv 17, NIV).

In other words, Abraham was saying unto God, "Lord you must be kidding. I am as old as dirt and Sarah is almost too old to remember her name, and you expect me to believe that Sarah will give birth to a child?" We have not slept together in years, the shop has closed long ago, and Sarah has passed the menopause stage, yet you are telling me that Sarah, my wife shall bear a child? Ha! Ha! Ha! Said, Abraham to himself.

God responded by saying, ***"Is anything too hard for the Lord? At the time appointed I will return unto thee, according to the time of life, and Sarah shall have a son"*** *(Genesis 18:14, NIV).* ***'And the Lord visited Sarah as he had said, and the Lord did unto Sarah as he had spoken."***

"For Sarah conceived, and bare Abraham a son in his old age, at the set time of which God had spoken to him." "And Abraham called the name of his son that was born unto him, whom Sarah bare to him, Isaac" (21:1-3).

On another occasion God did tempt Abraham. He said unto him, ***"Take now thy son, thine only son Isaac, whom thou lovest, and get thee into the land of Moriah; and offer him there for a burnt offering upon one of the mountains which I will tell thee of"*** *(22:2, NIV).*

Abraham did not say unto the God, "Lord Why Me, why must I sacrifice, the son whom I lovest? Instead he immediately took his son, Isaac, gathered wood for the burnt offering, got up, and went to the place where God told him to go"(vv 3, NIV).

Following God's instructions, he prepared the altar of sacrifice, laid Isaac upon it, took the fire in his hand and a knife, tied Isaac up, and stretched forth his hand in an effort to fulfill God's command (vv 3, 10, NIV).

God watched as Abraham prepared Isaac as a living sacrifice. He waited to see if Abraham would be disobedient. And after what seemed like forever to Abraham, God sent an angel instructing him not to lay a hand upon the lad.

Moses another servant of God, questioned God when he was given the assignment of leading the Israelites out of the land of Egypt. Moses said unto God, *"Who am I, that I should go unto Pharaoh, and I shall bring forth the children of Israel out of Egypt?"* (Exodus 3:11, NIV). God answered him by saying:

> *"Certainly I will be with thee; and this shall be a token unto thee: When thou hast brought forth the people out of Egypt, ye shall serve God upon this mountain"* (Exodus 3:12, NIV).

In other words, God was reassuring Moses that he would be with him during this assignment. He did not scold him for asking "Who do you think am I that I should go before Pharaoh the King of Egypt?"

Gideon, was called by God to set free Israel out of the hands of the Midianites, questioned his assignment:

> *"And he said unto him, Oh my Lord, wherewith shall I save Israel? behold, my family is poor in Manasseh, and I am the least in my father's house"* (Judges 6:15, NIV). *"And the Lord said unto him, Surely I be with thee, and thou shalt smite the Midianites as one man"* (vv 16, NIV).

God, again reassured him that he did not need to worry because He was going to be with him, guiding him through this tedious assignment. He did not yell, nor rebuke Gideon for questioning Him.

Evidently, Gideon was afraid of the Midianites and needed reassurance of the Lord, God before attempting to rescue Israel.

Saul, first king of Israel asked counsel of God, *"Shall I go down after the Philistines? wilt thou deliver them into the hand of Israel? But he answered him not that day."*

David, Israel's greatest and most admired king inquired of the Lord, saying:

> *"Saying, shall I go up to the Philistines? wilt thou deliver them unto mine hand? And the Lord said unto David, Go up: for I will doubtless deliver the Philistines into thine hand"* (II Samuel 5 : 19, NIV).

Elijah one of the greatest prophets of the Bible, told Ahab that there would be a drought, cried unto the Lord, and said:

O Lord my God, hast thou also brought evil upon the widow with whom I sojourn, by slaying her son? (I Kings 17:20, NIV)."And the Lord heard the voice of Elijah; and the soul of the child came unto him again, and he revived"(I Kings 17:22, NIV).

Elijah cried out to God in prayer concerning the widow woman who feed him while he was at Zarephath.

He questioned God about the evil that had fallen upon the woman's only child, and in doing so; God brought the widow woman's child back to life.

Jesus God's only begotten son, cried out to God asking, *"My God, my God why have thou forsaken me?"* (St. Mark 15:34, NIV).

Throughout the Bible we saw numerous people questioning God. Many of them enquired of God because of circumstances they were uncertain of. The prophets of Bible Days, sought clarity of duty, bringing a message to the people from God. Many lived their life as a mouth piece for God knowing they would be ostracized, persecuted or killed.

Their relationship with God provided insight for believers of modern day society. It is from their relationship with God that we are able to be comfortable when approaching the Lord, our Savior.

Christians must know who they are in Christ when questioning Him. In knowing who you are, opens doors for a deeper relationship with the Father. Our relationship with the Father allows us the same privileges as those of the Bible. We have been given the same rights as our forefathers. We have the ability of going to God in prayer with all of our concerns. His word declares, *"Ye have not, because ye ask not" (James 4:2, NIV).*

Therefore, as Christians we can go to God with all of our questions. It is not what we ask of Him that counts, but the manner in which we appeal to our Lord and Savior.

Our connections with God, dictates our willingness to advance towards Him when we are troubled by the things of life. We can ask Lord, Why Me? Why so much pain? We can ask and it shall be given unto us. This is a promise He has made in His Word. Therefore, when we are in need of answers to unanswered questions, we can go to our Fathers asking, Why so many heartaches? Why so much disappointment? Why so many tears? Why so many lies? Why so much suffering? Lord, why must I endure so much? Lord, Why me?

"I will say unto God my rock, why hast thou forgotten me? Why go I mourning because of the oppression of the enemy?" (Psalms 43:9, NIV).

2

A KISS OF BETRAYAL

Can you remember the first time your husband kissed you? Can you envision the touch of his lips, the stroke of his hands as he so gently embraced you, the warmth of his body as he pressed himself against you?

Yes, I can recall my first kiss as though it were yesterday.

The remembrance so sweet, as though it was a warm summer night.

Have you ever been kissed by someone who's motives were not genuine, only to have your heart broken. Have you eagerly given yourself and most of all your heart, only to find out it was not you that the person wanted?

Many times women are fooled by the look in a man's eyes, the smile on his face, and the words that he speaks. Some men are often times tricked by the smile on a woman's face, the movement of her hips, as she slowly struts off from him; the look of her lips, or the shape of her body.

A person may find themselves pushed into a relationship that was never meant to be by these seducing images. Both single and married couples find themselves trapped in a web of deception and betrayal.

When this happens, the person that entrusted their heart to the deceiver slowly realizes their world is suddenly coming to a halt. They are forced to face reality as it actually is. They find themselves angry, disappointed and ever so hurt. And oftentimes, they ask their mate, "What did I do to deserve this, how could you do this to me?"

Unlike Jesus, who was betrayed by Judas Iscariot, our reaction is not to deal with the situation from a spiritual point but from a natural view. Sometimes we minimize, rationalize, and penalize the person that has caused our hurt.

3

JUDAS ISCARIOT, SON OF SATAN

Judas Iscariot, one of the disciples and followers of Christ was most famous for his kiss of betrayal. He not only betrayed Jesus, but sold him for thirty pieces of silver.

Judas' motives appeared to be of a greedy nature. One day while Jesus dined with Lazarus and his family, Mary used an expensive bottle of perfume to wiped his feet, using her hair as a towel. Judas became so concerned over the cost of this perfume until he made a comment regarding it.

In his opinion, they could have made money from this expensive bottle of perfume. They could have sold it for *"Three hundred pence, and given the money to the poor" (John 12:6)*. But scripture shows he could care less about the poor.

On another occasion, Jesus spoke a parable to the disciples concerning his fate. However, none of them understood what it was He said unto them. The scripture declares in, John 13:21, Jesus became "Troubled in spirit and testified saying, Verily, verily, I say unto you, that one of you shall betray me."

However, the disciples did not believe Jesus, and in an effort to understand, Simon Peter asked, *"Who is it that would do such a thing?"* Jesus responded by saying, *"He it is, to whom I shall give a sop, when I have dipped it' and when he had dipped the sop, he gave it to Judas Iscariot, the son of Simon" (vv. 26, NIV)*.

During another conversation with the disciples, Jesus informed them that:

He was the living bread which came down from heaven: if any man eat of this bread, he shall live forever: and the bread that I will give is my flesh, which I will give for the life of the world (John 6:51, italic NIV).

Jesus realized that some of the disciples did not believe him and the scripture declares:

For Jesus knew from the beginning who they were that believed not, and who should betray him. And Jesus answered them, Have not I chosen you twelve, and one of you is a devil? *(John 6:64, 70 italic, NIV).*

The scripture states in Matthew 26:41:

Watch and pray, that ye enter not into temptation: the spirit indeed is willing, but the flesh is weak.

In other words, because the flesh is weak and is subject to sin, many believers may find themselves in situations very similar to that of Judas Iscariot.

Oftentimes, man's unwillingness to abstain from immoral acts leads him to commit treason against God. He tends to resort to things which are familiar such as drugs, alcohol and lustfulness of behavior which can cause deceit.

Deceit is a matter of respect and betrayal. It is a decision that consists of an immoral act against another person; and is based upon an individual's desire, to do or to have something that may or may not damage another person. Nevertheless, once a person has been deceived, an overwhelming feeling of betrayal always follows.

Deception and betrayal were not a part of God's plan for man's life. As a matter of fact, when these acts were committed, they assist in the aborting of God's purpose for man's life. God intend good for man, but our fleshly desires from the beginning of time has always interfered with God's plan for man.

Satan deceived Eve in the Garden of Eden when he twisted the very words of God leading her to believe that God had not meant what He said.

During their conversation, Satan the serpent, reversed the words of God by saying unto the woman, *"Yea, hath God said, ye shall not eat of every tree of the garden"?* *(Genesis 1:1, NIV).* Eve responded by saying:

> *"We may eat of the fruit of the trees of garden: But of the fruit of the tree which is in the midst of the garden God hath said, ye shall not eat of it, neither shall ye touch it, lest ye die" (Genesis 1:3, NIV).*

Satan, the serpent, said unto (the woman) Eve, *"You shall not surely die: For God doth (does) know that the day that you eat from this tree your eyes shall be opened, and you shall be as gods, knowing good and evil" (vv 4&5, NIV).*

As she looked at the fruit on the tree, curiosity overshadowed her. It was delightful to her eyes and her desire to taste the fruit was more than she could resist. As a result of being deceitful and disobedient to God, Adam and Eve succumbed to sin, causing death for themselves and everything that God had created.

Deceit take form in many shapes and when it is committed it causes betrayal. It should be avoided at all cost. Unlike the plan that God had for Jesus and Judas, the price of deception is not worth its expense.

Judas, betrayal to Jesus was apart of God's plan for the redemption of man. Jesus knew the plans that God had ordained for His life. In knowing his destiny, He recognized that He would be betrayed.

In fulfilling his duty to God and man, Jesus never complained about His obligations to His Father, nor did he discontinue his relationship with Judas. As a matter of fact, He successfully completed his task and lived a life consisting of no sin, nor faults. This was done as a token of his love to his Father and as an example for those who would followed after Him. Jesus did not deceive nor betray God nor man even when Satan tried tempting him in the wilderness after he had fasted for forty days and forty nights.

When man has been deceived or betrayed, his reactionsare much different than that of Jesus. He tend to rationalize the situation, examining it for understanding of what has happened, he becomes angry, bitter, desponded and sometimes cries because of the disappointment. Unlike man, Jesus never complained, grumbled, murmured or asked the question, Lord, Why Me? Instead it is written in the scripture that His very words were:

O my Father, if it be possible let this cup pass from me: nevertheless not as I will, but as thou wilt (St. Matthew 26:39, NIV).

4

TROUBLE IS IN THIS HOUSE

The Bible in its entirety is a book of history providing numerous examples of what took place during the lives of many Biblical characters.

Life for the modern day Christians does not appear to be that much different than that of Biblical folks.

The Bible depicts sin at its highest point, people were committing adultery on every end, fornication was a way of life as well, and we see lies, rape, murder and the worshipping of other gods.

For every problem and situation there was an answer.

However, many modern day Christians, are like those individuals in the Bible who did not look to God for resolution.

In today's society, trouble appears to be present on every end. There's trouble in our schools, churches, neighborhood, cities, towns, and in our homes.

People are plagued with financial hardship, we hear of "Wars and rumors of wars, mother's against daughters: fathers against sons, and nations against nations" (Matthew 24:6, NIV).

Our schools are overcrowded, cramped with students who aren't interested in learning. Their minds are loaded with junk which block their ability to focus. School is far from their mind and college is something they can never imagine.

Their family tree consists of one or two persons who have reached the pinnacle of their lives. Most members have settled for a lifestyle not compatible to what God has ordained. Poverty is a way of life that appears to be accepted by many.

Fathers are not present in many of our neighborhood homes, mothers are working two jobs and leaving their young ones alone. Young daughters are given the responsibility of raising their siblings, while most of them struggle to free themselves to a world of their own.

Our churches are filled with members who minds are not on God. They dress in their Sunday best, and do not know that their soul is not at rest. They serve as ushers, deacons, board members and sing in the choir; but yet they miss the little still voice of God that whispers in a cry, "My child do you not know, for you it was that I died."

Many preachers stand in the pulpit, ministering to people whom they betray. Even they themselves are fooled and have gone astray. They dress in robes of the cloth, while in their heart they do not strive to pray to a God who is faithful in all His ways.

Most of the time, many of them preach to a congregation, but yet they do not practice what they teach. They say they love God: and all the while they lay their head in the breast of the enemy. They cheat on God every chance they get, while in the pulpit they dress in their Sunday best.

Then there are those deacons who sit on the front pew of the church. Some so trapped by the wickedness of their mind, committing adultery and fornicating all of the time. In their heart they say, "It's okay to smoke a little dope, dance, party and drank a little wine and someday that woman will be mine."

Mother's of the church, many so bitter and angry sit watching their mate with hearts of hate as the younger females move about in search of a mate.

Choirs are filled with many, who sing songs of praise; yet they sing with their lips but, their love for God is far from their heart.

The person of the street, monitor the Christian and see his deceit. Most of them will not think about trading their seat. For they know that the so called Christian is hell bound. The street person is wise and practice what they preach, having wisdom of the things of this world, while the so called Christian is blinded to truth and think that he has fooled the one and only true living God. He has not fooled God, nor man, but has fooled himself.

Teenagers stand proudly gangster leaning on our neighborhood corners, having no sense of up bringing and no pride. Their clothes hang about their body as though they were rags: pants struggle to stay up on their behinds as the elderly look in disguise and nearly gag.

Young girls and boys are strapped with guns eagerly waiting to shoot and kill any one who get in their way. Confrontation and altercation are what they desire; and without thought, their aim is to shot you right between the eyes.

Drug addiction appears to be a part of every family tree. Sisters, brothers, sometimes fathers and mothers are hooked on a substance in which they can not afford. Drug addicted babies are born into a world having little chance of a normal life.

Crack cocaine is said to be a very poignant drug, so poignant until once a person has been drawn into its web, they become as a fly, trapped; having no means for escape. Many people have been enticed into trying this drug, only to find out they can not subdue it. Crack is so addicting until it will make a mother leave her home and leave her children all alone.

A pregnant woman will forget she is carrying a tiny little precious soul within. A father will sell his soul to conquer the demons within. It will make a person steal from him mother, father, sister and his brothers brother. It will make a preacher forget his sermon and a deacon to forget his wife.

This drug is reputed to have such an effect on a person until they will do anything to support their habit. Like

Satan, crack will cause a person to steal you blind; some it will kill; while others it will completely destroy just for succumbing to its wicked power.

I have never seen any one addicted to crack that would not sell everything he has. A husband will ask his wife to become his prostitute: a mother will sell her daughter to the first man that will have her, just to blow upon the holes in the cracks of that cocaine can.

A businessman, once hooked on crack will lose all that he has. He'll arrive at work late or he may not come at all.

He'll forget all of his business plans; sell his business for a mere ten dollar bill and even forget that he was a prominent figurehead.

Crack cocaine is such an addicting drug, it will make one forget he is a person of status. It captivates all that it conquers; turning them into a vagabond; causing them to forget to eat, drink, take a bath or change their clothes. It's so poignant that it will make a doctor sell his practice (just for a smell of the smoke from that crack cocaine can).

Those who succumb to its seducing powers lose all sense of judgment and will do anything to calm the raging lion within.

Alcohol is another addicting substance that alters the mind to the point of oblivious. Like crack cocaine it has also ruined the lives of numerous people.

As a child, I have witnessed the effects of alcohol and how it turns a home into a wreck. It is prevalent and takes its toll on nearly one out of ten homes in American. In some insidious way it can be just as harmful as crack. It is so common until family members turn their heads and look the other way, seeing no harm in its deluding savor.

I have seen skid rows and drunks all over the place, some of them I have seen lay on the street beneath the trees, in our parks, and under our neighborhood bridges.

Throughout our towns, you can see people, both young and old who's daily routine consist of hanging out at the community's corner store, the "House of Spirits," that is.

Some appear so intoxicated until their faces are distorted, their body posture slumped in a stupor, as many of them lay stretched out on our cities pavement.

Fathers, mothers, sometimes sisters and brothers walk the streets strutting about in a daze, having on no shoes while their clothes hang about their body in an unthinkable disarray.

Drug abuse, alcohol, financial hardship, and a life without Christ leads to numerous family problems, inflicting unforeseen trouble within our homes.

According to Job 14:1: "Man that is born of a woman is of a few days, and full of trouble" (NIV).

5

TROUBLE IS IN JOB'S HOME

Trouble can be seen in our homes and all over the land, even throughout the Bible, there was trouble on every hand. The Bible describes Job, as a man who was considered to be one of the most prominent and richest men of his time. He was a man of status, one who had it all. His household consisting of himself, his wife, seven sons and three daughters.

One day while *"The sons of God were presenting themselves before the Lord, Satan came among them"* *(Job 1:6, NIV).*

And the Lord asked him, *"Where are you coming from Satan? He responded by saying, "From going to and fro in the earth, and from walking up and down in it" (vv 7).*

God who is all knowing, everywhere and ever-present said unto Satan, *"Have you considered my servant Job, for there is none like him in the earth, for he is a perfect and upright man, one that feareth God and avoids sin" (vv 8).*

With this suggestion in mind, Satan set out to destroy Job and everything he owned. Satan said *"I shall touch everything that he hath and he will surely curse you to your face."*

God responded by saying give it your best shot, (my terminology) *"All that he hath is in your power; only upon himself put not thy hand.' And Satan left the presence of God" (vv 12, NIV).*

Satan immediately put forth his plan to sabotage Job's life. While Job looked out at all that God had given him, a servant came and informed him of the *"Sebeans that fell upon the oxen and the asses and killed all the servants and only he was left behind"* (vv 15, NIV).

If that was not enough, another servant came running to Job informing him that *"God sent a fire from heaven and burned up the sheep, the servants and consumed them leaving only one servant"* to tell the story (vv 16, NIV).

As Job listened with his head dropped and grief in his heart, yet came another servant, racing to tell him that, *"The Chaldeans who took off with three bands, fell upon the camels, and took them away and killed the servants with the edge of the sword; and only I escaped alone to tell thee"* (vv 17, NIV).

Soon afterward, Job received the worst news of all. A servant informed him that the children that he had been praying for were all dead. The house in which his sons and daughters were partying suddenly fell upon them and they were killed.

Job became so despondent until *"he took off his mantle, shaved his head, fell down to the ground and worshipped the Lord"* (vv 20, NIV).

Satan went back before the presence of the Lord, and the Lord said unto him, *"Job has held strong to his integrity"* and has not turned away from me? (Job 2:3, NIV).

Satan answered by saying, *"Skin for skin, yea, all that a man hath will he give for his life. Put forth thine hand now, and touch his bone and flesh, and he will curse thee to thy face"* (vv 4, 5, NIV).

Satan immediately went out and caused sores to form upon Job's body. Yet, Job never cursed God. He aggressively held to his integrity. However as Job's wife witnessed his affliction, she went to him advising him *"to curse his God and die"* (vv 9, NIV).

Throughout all of Job's trials and tribulation, suffering and affliction; up's and downs, never once did he relinquish his relationship with God. He vowed to himself, *"thou he slay me yet, will*

***I trust Him.*"** And as a result of his faithfulness to God, he was blessed twice the amount of every thing he lost.

Many times when Christians are challenged, they tend to make decisions that are detrimental to their destiny. They make decisions which are based according to the flesh, resulting in their shifting away from God and not trusting Him for their well-being.

When trouble comes, and it will come, the average Christian does not remember the scripture which reads in Roman 8:28 *(NIV, italics)*:

> ***We know that all things work together for good to them that love God, to them who are called according to his purpose.***

They somehow forget that God has a purpose for their life. In reality, they focus their attention on their problems, forgetting to put their trust in the Word of God. They seek other alternatives for solving their problems.

As a part of the cycle of life, we will be confronted with things un-becoming to us. Our faith in God must be tested.

When we are tested and pass the test of faith, it is at this point that we develop into Kingdom building material.

We must weather the storms of life, stay the course, stand up to the enemy while being covered with the Word of God. We must not abandon our faith.

If God does not allow our faith to be tested we would remain in our comfort zone, forfeiting our right to spiritual growth and maturity.

We must remember when trouble arrives, it is a test of faith, and is done because God is perfecting those things pertaining to us. However, it is at this point, where many believers succumb to sin, falling out of the will of God and betraying Him for the enemy.

In conclusion, Psalms 27: 5 declares, ***"For in the time of trou-***

ble he shall hide me in his pavilion: in the secret of his tabernacle shall he hide me; he shall set me up upon a rock."

6

A WOUNDED HEART

As I examined the chapters of my life, I began to think of times when I had been disappointed. Disappointed over someone else's behavior in the way they treated me. I thought about the many tears I have cried all because the people I loved and trusted saw no wrong in the acts that they committed against me. Of course not, for it was man that mistreated Jesus and saw no harm in the crime they committed against Him. So who am I and why should I be exempted?

Life for me has not been easy and has consisted of more heartaches and pain than I would care to remember. But with each tear I have had to cry and from every pain I felt, I now know that they came to push me into my destiny.

One night while having a pity party and after reminiscing over the hand that life had dealt me, I began questioning God as to why so many negative things happened to me during my life."

Looking at the pictures in my mind, I suddenly found myself emotionally overwhelmed and mentally exhausted over what I saw. This movie was much more than I could handle, so I started crying and praying. I went to the Bible for answers, because I realized that only God could help me. I found Biblical people who lives were very similar to mine. As a matter of fact, they were just like me, all messed up!

I read about the many men of the Bible who had countless women in their life. Adultery appeared to be running rampant throughout the Bible. Fornication had its place too. Even the angels of God, who were on assignment, they too sinned against Him.

I stumbled upon David's daughter Tamar who was raped by her brother, Amnon, and the problems David brought upon his household because of his lustfulness.

I read about a man who was tormented by demons, about the abuse the Israelites suffered as slaves, at the hands of Pharaoh.

After examining the scriptures, I began to understand the persecution of Jesus, the rejection he felt, the physical abuse given Him on Calvary, the betrayal of Judas and the denying by Peter.

I was somewhat comforted in learning that maybe I had been set aside as an example and for a testimony to others facing similar problems. My hope began to arise as I was able to ascertain Biblical methods for overcoming my problems. I slowly saw how the enemy device traps to trick God's children and the many mind games he plays.

Satan used my mind in such a harsh manner, reflecting upon all of life's tragedies, until I could barely see the goodness of God. He took my mind on a journey where it traveled through a town called "Heart Break City". In this town, I was introduced to "Captain Rejection, Lieutenant Confusion, Sergeant Bitterness and Colonel Disappointment."

After meeting each of them, I watched the events of my life as it was told and every buried memory became unraveled. Reliving chapters of abandonment, abuse, neglect, sexual assaults and rejection was more than my mind could bear. I became depressed, despondent and suicidal.

As my mind traveled through this emotional landmine, my thoughts landed me in every ditch, trench, on top of rough mountains and many steep hills, when all of a sudden it came to a crashing halt, a spirit of suicide tried to attach it self to me.

Years later, I realized once my mind was opened that Satan tried taking advantage of this situation, by subjecting it to all types of evil thoughts. He began showing me the events of my parent courtship as well as the breakup of their marriage. He tried to convince me that I was an illegitimate child and that I was the product of an illusive affair, but legal documents proved otherwise.

As I slowly glanced through these images, they were at first a bit overwhelming. But I needed closure to unanswered questions, so I pressed forth in an effort to understand. When I was finally told what took place between my parents, I could not help but ask, "Lord, Why me"? How could any innocent child become entrapped in the midst of their parents bitter dispute? To my surprise, God answered me by saying:

> ***Before I formed thee in the belly I knew thee; and before thou camest forth out of the womb I sanctified thee* and I ordained thee a prophet unto the nations** *(Jeremiah 1:5, NIV).*

It was now understandable what God's purpose was for my life. All of a sudden, I realized that my parents were mere vehicles used by God for bringing me into this world. God had plans for my life which I could not see at that time due to the many heartaches and pain I suffered throughout life.

Looking over the issues of my parent life, and watching as the sins of my father were passed down to his children, my life-story began to make sense. The tears had become lesser and lesser until they are no more.

As a married woman, I could now understand the hurt and pain of my mother as she embraced the rejection of my father. I imagined how belittled she must have felt as she watched him walk away, hand in hand, with another woman. Pregnant and abandoned by her husband, how sad she must have felt.

It was apparent his desire was not to be her husband because he was in love with another woman. With her hurt and pain, my

Lord, Why Me?

mother packaged her bags, gathered her belongings and walked away from the marriage, never looking back.

My mother slowly began to put the pieces of her life back together, and like my father this would not include me. I would eventually be raised by her oldest sister and her husband, Annie Wees and Uncle Accie.

As a child, I could not understand why neither of my parents wanted me. I was their first. No one told me that I was not wanted, it was what I concluded. I did not feel loved by either of them.

I would spend a portion of the summer with my father, an occasion I enjoyed. This was an opportunity to be with and learn more about my half siblings. They were always glad to see me. The time spend together was great. There were eight of them and I was always curious about the circumstances surrounding their birth.

I wondered if they were experiencing the same types of mishaps as I. Each time I visited Daddy he was always intoxicated. I can recall visiting him one summer with my children. When we arrived to his home, he was sprawled out on the side walk outside his house dead drunk. This made a lasting impression of him in the mind of his grandchildren.

As I grew up and things began to happen that negatively affected my life, I soon realized that the Spirit of Rejection had transferred itself upon me from my mother's womb.

As a youngster, I could always feel the presence of this spirit. This spirit appeared to be the Captain of all other spirits visiting me. Oftentimes it brought with it the spirit of confusion. My mind would move from sane to nearly insane in trying to analyze why I was not wanted. [I could not understand why my Father did not want me as he did his other children; especially since I was his first born.]

This spirit would bring several friends with him, the spirit of envy, jealousy and division. As a young adult, I would later see the other woman's envy and observe her hurt as I looked into her eyes.

In her mind, I no doubt was a constant reminder of my father's sexual relationship with my mother and his rejection to her. I began to feel as though I was in the middle of a Jacob's, Leah and Rachel's battle. And somehow I had become Joseph.

One day while visiting my Dad, she said to me, as we conversed with each other "that I never came around until I wanted money." It was at this point that I started to realize that she was envious and jealous of me. And as a result of our conversation, my father did not see me for several years, for I refused to return to his home.

Living with my aunt and uncle was wonderful. We did all the things that a family does together. We ate at a certain time, had small family discussions during mealtimes. We were disciplined when we did wrong and most of all we were taught the importance of loving and serving God. My belief in God came from this household.

My aunt was an evangelist who had a very strong belief in God. Out of all the people that I had known, she was the only person that had been saved all of her life. She instilled that which was right in the sight of God into my skull. She preached and taught us about the love of God and she was determined not to let us be lost to the world.

However, at age twelve, I decided that I wanted to live with my mother. It was in this house, Satan tried destroying me. He submitted all sorts of foul spirits upon me. In this house, Satan was having a field day. It appeared as though this was his campground and He stationed every demon that he had there. He had in position a lust demon, an abusive demon, a confused demon, a drunk demon and a sex demon. Like Tamar, David's daughter this sexual demon took pry on me. While living with my mother, I was sexually abused by three different males on three different occasions.

The last rape was so severe until, I was sure this rapist was going to kill me, but the voice of God came to me instructing me on how to react. Obeying the voice of God, I survived this ordeal but not without physical and mental scars. This was the beginning of my hearing the voice of the Lord.

Mentally I was a mess, all torn up inside, afraid of every male I saw, except for my immediate family members. Day after day, I resorted to crying, trying over and over again to understand why these bad things happened to me.

In an effort to understand and to fill a void in my life, at age sixteen, I married the first guy that showered me with love and affection. Being young and foolish, and not understanding the game of love, I became his bride and the mother of his first born child, a decision I later came to regret (marriage that is).

Life with him was nothing in comparison to that of my uncle and aunt. Their home consisted of comfort, stability and love. And "Beat Em' Up" (the name that I shall call him) house, which was supposed to become my home was centered a round much physical abuse.

After we were married, he became insanely jealous for no apparent reason of every male that said anything to me, or looked at me. He was so enraged with jealousy, he went as far as accusing me of entering a sexual relationship with my mother's twin brother, who was my favorite uncle. My life with him was a living nightmare and consisted of receiving numerous beatings on a daily basis.

We were married on September 19, this was to be the happiest day of our lives; however, as it turned out, it was one of the worst moments of my life. It was the beginning of another nightmare. Our honeymoon consisted of working on the farm, feeling the full effects of the suns rays picking tomatoes.

I can recall the soreness of my knees as I knelt on the rough sandy ground beside numerous rows of tomatoes. As if this was not enough, we bought our four month old infant child along. The child laid quietly under the small vines of tomatoes for shade.

Little did I know that our livelihood would come from working as farmers, nor had I anticipated the change of seasons which would affect our income. All of a sudden reality stepped in, winter hurriedly approached us, and we were both un-educated teenagers with no money.

I married "Beat Em' Up," thinking I could get away from the craziness that I entertained while living with my mother. I could not understand why confusion was every where I went. Confusion, bitterness, jealousy, partying and alcohol were not hear of in my uncle and aunt's home. I began having problems functioning mentally, because of this.

From the start, my mother disapproved of the marriage and refused to assist us in any way. She evidently saw that he was abusive and wanted to shield me. One day while I was hanging clothes on the line out back, she walked up on him as he was choking me. This enraged her, but I had to have him, I loved him. I loved Beat Em' Up so much until if I had gone to the doctor and he had told me it was okay to eat ten links of his poop, I would have eaten fifteen more links. My mother's philosophy was "If you make your bed hard, then sleep in it." And my God, did she stick to her decision.

"Beat Em' Up," immediately applied for welfare and food stamps for the three of us, and was accepted. There were days when I went without food. Beat Em' Up had a gambling problem and did not use the funds properly. Month to month, I found myself worrying about not having the basic necessities of life.

Beat Em' Up did not believe in working. It was the last thing on his mind. Night after night, he would result to the streets, telling me that he was hustling. Hustling was all that he knew and he was aspiring to be a "big time hustler."

The problem that I had with that theory was he never brought anything home after being out all night. He always came home broker than when he left.

When I could no longer sit back and watch him squander away

the check, I reported him to the Welfare and Food Stamps authorities and they gave me the check.

Years later, I realized history was repeating itself, and I would be following in the same footsteps of my mother, who also was a welfare recipient. After spending three long years on welfare and waking up to a rude awakening, along with numerous beatings, I tried leaving the relationship.

It was not easy leaving this relationship, I loved Beat Em' Up and my emotions were entangled around him like a fly caught in a huge spider web. Not only was I in an emotional boo-be trap, he always found me when I left him.

He would watch me from a distant, following me around, constantly calling until I gave in to his demands.

The saddest thing I remembered was taking him back, no matter how badly I was beaten. He had such a pity demon which always made me feel sorry for him. Sometimes he would cry telling me how much he loved me. Oh, how pitiful he could look for what he had done to me. The look of sadness on his face, the pleading of mercy in his voice as he begged for forgiveness; always promising never to hit me again, but he did. After the beatings, the making up was always so sweet. Looking back, I think I looked forward to making up after being beaten. For this was the only time he appeared to be in love with me.

I can recall on one occasion after taking him back how he beat me for no unknown reason. As he hit me over and over again, tearing fire to my behind, I quickly felt the flames as they ignited my skin, suddenly I sensed the need to escape this violence. Looking around the room, and seeing no place to escape. I made a wild dash out of our second floor apartment window, into a leap of freedom.

As I shot pass him like a bolt of lightning, through the window in which he stood in front of, he glanced out at me with disbelief in his eyes and watched as I hit the ground below. Out of fear of him, I struggled to get up: hoping to run for my life, but to my surprise, I could not get up. My right foot had been broken and was dragging like a dog's foot that had been run over by a car.

I landed on the crisp ground below, moaning and groaning like a sick puppy, my girlfriend heard my cries and realized what had happened to me. She rushed to my aide and made a call to my mother. My mother immediately arrived to our house. When she approached me and saw the condition that I was in, she turned to Beat Em' Up, who took flight like a scald dog, leaving me in pain, anguish and ashamed to fin for myself.

My mother upon seeing me was steaming over what had happened. As she questioned me, you could see the steam from the smoke as it slowly rose from her ears and nose.

She took me to the hospital. It seemed as though hours ticked by as we sat patiently in the hospital emergency room.

My foot was swollen like a balloon and felt as though every bone in it was shadowed. When the physician finally made his rounds, he was totally surprised as to what had happened. I slowly explained to him what took place between me and Beat Em' Up. His last words to me were, "You are a very lucky young lady; you could have killed yourself."

I told him, I thought I was going to die, so I decided to run and having no place to escape, the second floor window was my only way out. Upset over what had happened to me and seeing the disgust on my mother's face, I went home with her.

After a few days, I started to miss Beat Em' Up. He began calling, begging and pleading for forgiveness. And as always, I was like a dog with a new bone, "a sucker." I packed my belongings and left without saying a word to my family.

My mother was livid when she found out I had return home to Beat Em' Up. [In her heart, she knew that one day he would either beat me to death or accidentally give me a blow to the body that

Lord, Why Me?

would eventually kill me.] I didn't care, all I knew was "I loved him and he loved me," and I missed him.

Shortly after going home, I again found myself in trouble. I was pregnant with our second child and the romance was over. This man started acting like a maniac, he would fly into a rage for no apparent reason and with each mood change he would beat the crap out of me. He began fussing, cussing and accusing me of things I had not done.

All of a sudden he started sending vicious blows to my body. I fell to the floor in an effort to shield myself. As I lay in a fetus position to cover my body and our unborn child, he began stomping a mud hole out of me. As his feet hovered over my pregnant body, a pimp rushed to my rescue and said to him. "Man stop that, that is no way to treat a lady." He pushed him off of me, and on his command the kicking stopped.

This time, I did not have nerves enough to go home to my mother, instead he made me sleep outside our apartment in the hallway. I stayed there all night into the next day. The weather was inclement and I felted as though I was going to freeze to death. But like always, we made up and I took him back or should I say he allowed me to come back into our house.

However, after taking him back, things did not get any better between us. The beatings were more frequent and always without cause.

Several months later, between the hours of three thirty to four in the morning, I was awaken to the echoing of his fist as it shattered my head. It was as though he had lost his mind and for no apparent reason, he placed a knife around my throat. Just as he was attempting to slit my throat, God sent one of my friends to our home, who knocked on the door, stopping this horrendous act. This was my last and final beating that I received from him. I hurriedly left this house with my friend, going to a land of no return. I left him and never looked back.

As I rushed away on that early spring morning, I left the children with Beat em' Up. I was so glad to be alive and away from him until I forgot my children. I had no idea he would threaten to harm them if he could not have me. After calling all around town trying to find me, and unable to do so, he called my boss informing him of his intent of burning down our home with the children in it, if I did not return home.

I was terrified of him and had to get the police to get my children. He was hot as a thirty eight when I arrived with the law. No one believed me when I said it was over, especially my family.

Beat Em' Up would physically abuse me and my uncles would beat him up, but this did not stop the beating. Finally, I had had enough. The ordeal with the knife to my throat woke my happy tail up and I did not go back to him. I divorced him with sorrow in my heart.

Although, I knew he was no good for me, it took years of heartaches, pain and suffering for me to get over him. Five long years I longed for him, even while being married to my second husband.

Beat Em' Up refused to allow me out of his life just like talking about it. He would follow me wherever I moved. If I relocated to South Florida, within a few days he would be spotted lurking around the corner where I lived. If I moved back up north, shortly afterwards, he would be seen standing on the corner watching me.

Beat Em' Up followed me around for nearly eighteen years, until he was forced into realization that I had no intentions of ever being his wife again. When he finally realized it was over, he said to me that "He cared more about a damn dog than he did our children."

This was the straw that broke the camels back. I walked away from him never speaking to him for a number of years. I never had peace knowing this man was following me around like butter on bread.

After comprehending that we were never going to live together as husband and wife, Beat Em' Up turned to a lifestyle of a vagabond, sleeping under bridges, in abandoned cars and turning to a life of drugs and making a career out of going in and out of jail.

Proverbs 18:14 declares: *"The spirit of a man will sustain his infirmity; but a wounded spirit who can bear (NIV)?*

7

A BROKEN HEART

I meet "Cheater John" shortly after leaving "Beat Em' Up." My friends and I had gone out for a night on the town at a local "juke joint" in the next town. Before meeting Cheater, my friends encouraged me to write to him while he was residing in another city, but I refused because I was still married to Beat Em' Up. They told me everything about him, his personality, his smile, the way he looked and most of all, he was a street fighter. They painted a picture of him in my mind but it was too vague. When we finally met I did not recognize him. He was tall, slender and light in complexion and was not quite what I was wanted in a man.

    We talked and laughed the night away and after talking and dancing for several hours, I felt safe and comfortable being in his company. I had not dated anyone but Beat Em' Up, and due to being raped I was very afraid of the opposite sex. I did not trust them for fear of being sexually assaulted again. Cheater was different, having such a sense of humor and he was charming as well. After talking for a minute we decided to date each other. He was not the type of guy that I had in mind, but what the heck I thought, he would at least protect me from the brutal beatings of Beat Em' Up. I was taken in by his kindness and his deep sense of humor, along with his vow to keep me from being harmed, something I very much needed.

    After a short courtship, Cheater John and I began living together as husband and wife even though we did not have a marriage license. Our life consisted of experimenting with drugs, having numerous wild parties and just running around like a bunch of wild animals.

We lived together approximately three years before deciding to make it legal. At which time, we moved to New York: where things began to change. It was there that we ceased using illegal drugs and having all kinds of wild parties. Life with him was not as challenging as it was with Beat Em' Up, my first husband, but it did have its problems.

In this marriage, I was hit, but not as much. Finally, I made a choice and decided that I was not going to stay in any relationship where I was being physically abused and he never hit me again.

Cheater John informed me of the things he would do. He said, "He did not like to work, he loved getting high and most of all, he loved women." His exactly words to me were, "I will screw a rattle snake if you hold his head, I'll screw them from eight to eighty, blind, cripple or crazy, dead or alive," he loved woman. Cheater John also informed me that he could not have children.

After being together for several months I found myself pregnant. Cheater John had convinced me that he could not have children. Like some nut, I stopped taking my birth control pills and found myself pregnant with his first child. He had not lied, he could not give birth to a child, but I could.

Cheater John was a person who loved to get high and party. One Friday night he decided to go out on the town, not returning until the following Monday morning. I was steaming and made up my mind to run away from him.

I called my mother and asked her if she would give me train fare so that I could move back to New York. She went off, but nevertheless she wired me the money. I rushed home, packaged my children and my belongings and was praying to be gone by the time Cheater came home. However, my plans did not take place as I wished. Someone in the neighborhood told him I was trying to skip town on him and he broke his neck getting home. When Cheater got home, he had his money in hand and was ready to move. I informed him that I didn't know how my mother would feel about me bringing a boyfriend home to live in her house, so he called her. To my surprise she invited him to New York.

After moving to New York, we had to stay with her for a couple of months. Like the first marriage, we worked on the farm for a living picking all sorts of crops. We picked tomatoes, potatoes, blue berries, and strawberries and a portion of our money went towards purchasing marijuana.

Our friends were exactly like us. I guess you could say "Birds of a feather, flock together," they too were a bunch of "pot heads." Every day we would buy an ounce of weed. We would party until the break of dawn, getting up in time to go on the farm.

Cheater John never missed a party. Our weekends consisted of bar hopping. I was trying to be hip in keeping up with my cousins and sister-in –law. I had become accustomed to running the street like every body else. The only thing about my running the street, I would always end up praying wherever we went. I would ruin our house parties by crying out to God while getting high.

One night while having a dope party, the twelve o'clock whistle blew. This whistle blew so loud until it scared the dickens out of me. I thought it was "Gabriella blowing his trumpet." I jumped up with my arms extended in the air, shouted "Father, God in the name of Jesus, have mercy on us, forgive us Lord! Every one in the room looked at me: as though I was crazy and said to one another "man she is always praying and blowing our high." I immediately sit down petrified to participate anymore that night.

Those parties would always include the opposite sex. Cheater John would be the life of the party as well as a big flirt. Women loved him and I hated them. I would end up watching him like a hawk, trying to sabotage his plans of getting with some of them.

However, the inevitable happened, Cheater John had become

Lord, Why Me?

involved with a female that lived around the corner from us. Mama stayed around the corner too, and on this particular day, I decided to pay her a visit. When I turn the corner, I heard Bump call out to me saying "Ooh Bonnie let me tell you about Cheater John and Gayle." I was devastated when she finished her story. I slowly walked back around the corner, never reaching my Mother's house. I was shaken up, hurt and mad.

He too was rejecting me. I began crying hysterically to the point of not being able to stop. I lost my mind within a split second. I could not focus. My mind was spinning in circles and nothing made sense to me from that point on. In many ways life had been so unkind to me and my mind could no longer handle the over load.

I had become depressed and despondent over life issues.

Before I knew it, a whirlwind of emotions had overshadowed me. My mind began drifting like a ship without a sail. Thoughts of suicide dropped into my spirit as though they were an anchor.

As my mind sailed out to sea, I found myself in deep troubled waters. When my ship finally came to rest, I was dazzled standing in front of our medication cabinet, holding a glass filled with a mixture of pills.

Tears gushed from my eyes like a river of water and the pain from all the years of abuse launched me into a suicidal mode. Satan, the Adversary said to me, "Drink it, drink all of it, for when you do; you will never cry again. You will never ever have to worry again."

Listening to the voice of the enemy and unable to see my way out of this hostile environment, I digested this poisonous substance as if it were a soft drink. Within minutes this drink began to take affect upon me. My body slowly crept into a relaxed mode and my mind laps from past to future. Not recognizing the signs of death, I laid sprawled on the bathroom floor as death slowly tipped my way.

All of a sudden, I heard cries, screams and footsteps rushing my way. I felt the pushing of the door and the voices of nervous people as they picked my limp body up from the floor and sped off to a local hospital.

In a muffled voice, I could hear my sister- in law telling someone, "This fool has tried to kill herself." When my family finally arrived at the emergency room, the doctor motioned for one of the nurses to slap me in the face nonstop. I heard him say to her, "don't let her go to sleep, she's ten minutes away from death."

After the doctor evaluated me to determine if I had all of my marbles, he sent my happy tail straight to the "nut' unit (psychiatric ward) that is.

Once admitted to this mental unit, I was placed in a locked room which had only a peak hole. I was allowed to have my cigarettes, but I was not allowed any matches. I thought to myself, "Who is crazy here?" 'They allowed me to have cigarettes, but no matches."

As I lay in bed in this mental institution listening to patients as they screamed out in terror, I thought to myself, "Why am I here? I'm not crazy." I witnessed one patient constantly banging her head on the wall and as a result of this, her bed had to be taken out of the room. She was placed on the floor with a mattress only. Another patient briskly walked the halls twirling his fingers while talking to himself. Several other patients moved about the room clothed in straight jackets while others were either tied to the chair or their bed.

On the next day, my family decided to pay me a visit. While they were there, my favorite cousins, Dee Dee said to me, "Bonnie if you eat the 37th chapter of Psalms, you will never end up in this crazy house again." Not knowing what she meant, I grabbed the Bible, opened it up, ripped out that chapter, chewed it up and swallowed that scripture as though I were a Billy goat. Everyone in the room looked at me in shock without saying a word.

Lord, Why Me?

On the next day my family decided to take me out for a walk in the corridors of this psychiatric unit. They noticed me walking around with newspaper on my feet and rubber bands around the ankles, as shoe lace. They asked me, "Bonnie, why are you walking around with that newspaper on your feet?" I responded by saying, they are my shoes, my feet are cold." This was when they realized that I was really delirious.

I later learned what Dee Dee meant when she told me to eat the scripture. What she meant was if I allowed the Word of God to penetrate my mind, and to come into my heart; His Word would become alive on the inside of me and protect me from all evil. I would be dressed in the whole armor of God. The helmet of salvation would cover my mind, the breastplate of righteousness my heart, the shod of the feet, the shield of faith and the Word that I ate up would be the Spirit that would watch over me. I needed help and I needed it in a hurry.

A few days go by, and the physician paid me a visit. He noticed that I was constantly crying over what had happened to me during my childhood. I especially could not forget the rapes. It was like a bad movie constantly replaying in my head. To help me forget my past he suggested I take a number of "Shock Treatments."

At that time, I did not know what those treatments entailed, but later learned that a portion of my brain would be electrocuted. After discussing his suggestion with my family, my mother hit the ceiling. She totally disagreed with this doctors choice of treatment. She believed I was already "too crazy" and these treatments would only make me crazier.

Nevertheless, I went to God in prayer. I asked Him to guide me with the decision I had been given and to heal my mind. After praying, I decided to take three treatments, one in the name of "The Father, The Son and The Holy Ghost."

Taking these treatments caused my memory to become very foggy and cloudy. I could barely remember my immediate family.

Somehow I had forgotten everyone, including my neighbors. But as time passed, I began to feel better about myself and decided to sign myself out of that that hospital. The doctor was upset with me over my decision to sign out against medical advice, but nevertheless I checked out of that hospital and went home.

Months after being released, things appeared to be going well between Cheater John and me. He began staying home more instead of going out with his friends. We were having less marijuana parties because everyone was concerned over my state of mind. They were afraid of me and I could not understand why.

However, when it appeared I was alright mentally, we started partying with our friends again. Cheater John went out with his friends and me with mines. As fate would have it, we somehow ended up at the same tavern in Pennsylvania.

As the females and I entered this tavern, Shirley, Cheater John's sister shouted, "Ooh, look at Cheater." Glancing around the room, looking from table to table, I could not see him. However, I knew from the sound of "Ooh" something was wrong.

The lights were dimmed, the music was groove and the entire room had the feel of romance. Couple lined the dance floor wrapped in each other arms like water in a sponge. All of a sudden I spotted Cheater John locked in the arms of another female.

I made my way to that dance floor like a bolt of lightning. I must have pecked on Cheater John's shoulder for about three minutes before he looked up. He was into the music and this girl. He had his arms wrapped tightly around her, if she wanted to get away it would have been nearly impossible. Cheater John was in grid lock, he was humping and bumping, stomping and grinding, lost in ecstasy and was doing the "bow hog grind" right before my very eyes.

When he looked up at me, his snake eyes became the size of a fifty cent piece. He said to me, "Let me explain Bonnie," but I refused to listen. I made my way off of that dance floor with my hand in my purse.

I was trying to load his thirty eight that I had been carrying around. God was on my side as well as his, because the holes in the gun chamber would not accept the bullets; somehow they had gotten smaller, not allowing me to load that gun.

I was a mad sister, and wanted my clothes off of that Negro's back. The shirt he wore, I bought it. The pants he had on, I purchased them. The socks he wore, they belonged to me as well as the shoes on his feet, they too were mine. All I wanted to do that night was make him undress, out of my clothes.

Cheater John did not come home for about a month. At which time he decided to make a change in the way he was living. This change would mean going to church, fasting, and praying and trying to convert all of his friends into becoming a Christian. I wasn't quite ready to change. Plus I did not trust him. How could he stop partying, smoking dope and become religious?

I was taught to worship God and had done that all of my life. My aunt constantly preached to me about getting save; yet I wasn't ready. I was willing to read the Bible to Cheater on those nights he came home high as a "Florida Kite," but living totally for the Lord was out of the question.

Cheater was making changes in his life and these plans would include leaving me, but he stayed with me a little longer out of guilt. By this time we were expecting our second child.

For a number of years, I was not bothered with sickness of mind, and things were well between me and my husband. I guess this is why he stayed a little longer and did not leave me.

We purchased our first home, a large two story house that included a full size attic. During the same year, we bought a brand new Lincoln Town car.

Within a few years, we decided to move to Florida in search of a better life. However, this move did not enhance our marriage;

instead it pushed us farther apart. With four small children and no formal education, we were struggling to make ends meet. I decided to enroll in the community college.

Cheater John was not pleased with this decision, but I went anyway. After three long years, I finally graduated with an Associate of Science Degree in Dietetic Technology from Palm Beach Community College. In my mind, I believed furthering my education would afford us an opportunity to improve the way we were living. However, I was wrong; he did not feel the same as I.

Instead he became envious and angry distancing himself from me. I guess you could say that the pressure of marriage had taken its toll on our relationship.

As he had done during the past, he took shelter in the arms of another woman. I became so involved in obtaining an education until I did not see any signs until it was too late. His desire was not to be with me.

Everyday our children tried telling me that their Daddy had a girlfriend. They would tell me about his phone calls that they over heard, yet I refused to listen to them. I could not afford to be distracted. I wanted an education more than anything in the world. Therefore, I was not going to let a mingle affair stop me.

My children were devastated when they saw their Dad with his girlfriend. They were even more hurt when he decided to leave the marriage. They began acting out in ways I could have never envisioned. I could not help them because I was struggling to maintain my sanity, leaving them to fin for themselves. As I let my children take care of themselves, they began wandering too far from the nest; and in doing so, they, were adventuring into un-familiar territories.

Our son began getting into all sorts of trouble. He could not be trusted around anyone because he had fingers like glue and therefore any thing that he touched would some how walk away with him.

Lord, Why Me?

Our baby girl started running away from home. I could not keep up with her even when I tried finding her. There were moments when she would be hiding and watching me as I searched in vain. She had began to hang out at the dance hall and I could not keep up with her. Out of all our children, I knew within my spirit that our breakup would have the most affects on her and it did. She became overly angry and upset. She was the most difficult of all the children to handle.

Our baby boy stayed mostly to himself. I guess he was too young to understand what had happened. He was a "mama's boy." I did not have that much trouble out of him. He remained with me until he was twenty one verses the other children who left home by the time they were fifteen. I tried keeping them in control as best I could but I was losing them to the streets. Once Cheater deserted us, he did not call nor come around. I needed help but had no where to turn.

I could not help my children, my mind was too fragile. Everything appeared to be nerve racking for me. My nerves were so shattered until I could barely function, I couldn't eat or sleep. In this incoherent world of mine, I was totally lost because my love life was a mess.

I had spent thirteen long years with this man and I was devastated over his decision to leave us. My mind could not take being rejected and I thought of committing suicide again. This time a little voice came to me telling me to kill the children first, then myself.

This voice would always talk to me. It would tell me things before they happened. It would tell me when a person was sick and what their condition was. It would tell me when someone was going to die. This was the voice that constantly tried convincing me to kill myself. This voice would converse with me trying to get me to do things beyond my power, but I would not. I would pray instead.

I prayed and prayed during this ordeal and was able to get through it without bringing harm to myself or our children. But I would struggle with this voice for years. This voice had become my little friend, talking with me on a regular basis.

During Cheater John's first attempt to leave me, I became so mentally deranged, until I had to be admitted into a mental ward of a hospital. On his last attempt to leave me I lost thirty pounds in a two weeks time frame. I was so frail until I looked like death on a walking cane. My friends and family thought I was on crack. Life experiences had taken its toll on me.

I found myself crying daily over my parents inability to accept me, the sexual abuse I endured as a child, the physical abuse I received as an adult, the breakup of my first marriage, and the hurt of knowing that my husband was an adulterer.

I was extremely hurt over this breakup due to the manner in which it happened. This affair was different; it took place in the "House of God." The pastor saw nothing wrong with his elders committing such an act in the house of God and especially against God.

As a matter of fact, once this pastor discovered that Cheater John and I had separated, he called my house late one night asking me out on a date. I could not believe my ears. How could he stand in God's pulpit preaching the Gospel every Sunday yet not live according to the Word of God?

I was angry over both their behavior. There were moments when I would become so upset over this separation until I could not function mentally. My mind would rehearse our life together over and over again. I could not make sense of what had going wrong. I would become so depressed until I would leave my job: arriving at his girlfriend house, sitting out front of her house with my middle finger protruding in the air for hours, hoping someone would have at least sneezed on me.

Early one Friday morning, I received a call from his lover

Lord, Why Me?

pleading with me to sign the divorce papers. She said she loved him and I guess; I must have felt sorry for her. I did not want to stand in the way of her happiness, so I gave my husband over to her on a silver platter.

After talking with her, I somehow made my journey back to reality, only to learn that my fifteen year old daughter Kesia, was expecting her first child. I became totally upset over this news because history was repeating itself. At age thirty three, I was being forced to become a grandmother: as so was the case with my mother.

In conclusion, according to Psalms 69:2:

Reproach hath broken my heart; and I looked for some to take pity, but there was none: and for comforters, but I found none.

8

A DECEITFUL HEART

In an effort to keep my sanity, I began looking for love in all the wrong places. After Cheater John and I separated, I tried dating, but the men I came in contact with wanted one thing; and, one thing only, and that was sex. I wasn't about casual sex. Sex was meant for love in my eyes.

I did not like the men I dated and decided against that. Instead, I focused my attention on developing my career and leaving the State of Florida. My goals were to move back up north with my family. I had no reason to stay, plus I was definitely not going to rekindle the relationship with Cheater.

My Mom lived in the house that Cheater and I purchased before moving to Florida. I would not have the worry of trying to find a place to stay for me and my children.

As a student at Palm Beach Community College, majoring in their Dietetic program we were assigned various places to complete our internship. My teacher picked the Mental Health Center for me to complete my area of study. Upon hearing my location, I became very upset. I did not want to go near that place. I had had enough of mental institutions. However, I went and successfully concluded my degree. I was such a good student until they asked to stay on for a few weeks more, working as a Diet Clerk.

Carrie, the Food Service Director was planning a month long vacation and someone was needed to operate the dietary department. I was offered an interim position during her absence, but

Lord, Why Me?

was not sure if I was going to remain in Florida or if I was relocating back to New York.

The thought of operating a food service department sounded great to me. I was nervous and not sure if I was capable of managing that department, but I was eager to put my new skills to work. I felt comfortable with the staff because, they were the ones that had trained me during my internship. There were approximately fifteen associates employed at the Center, of the fifteen; Dona Trust and I hit it off.

It would be Dona' Trust whom I would confide in about my decision to leave Florida and about taking the temporary position at the center. Dona' encouraged me to accept the position and asked me to stay in Florida as well. However, I had a problem; I needed to move from the house where Cheater and I lived. My income was not sufficient enough to afford the mortgage. When Cheater abandoned me and the children, he rarely contributed funds toward their care. Therefore, moving was a priority on my list. I had never been evicted before and did not want that happening now. Dona' asked me to stay, promising to find a place for me and my children to reside. I agreed providing he found a nice place in a good neighborhood.

Within a week Dona' Trust found a big beautiful three bedroom two bathe home. This house had a nice front and back yard, with a fence around it. When I saw it, I loved that house and decided not to move back to New York.

Trusting his judgment, I accepted the offer and became employed at the Dialysis Health Center, as their Dietary Manager and I remained in the State of Florida. This would be the beginning of a new chapter in my life story. It would be the place where I would meet the love of my life.

Dona' Trust was already employed at the Dialysis Health Center and was moving about life as though he had it going on. We became good friends, talking about everything under the sun.

Most of our discussions were about past relationships. We did not give much thought to our conversations, however; something was beginning to transpire between us. I found myself waiting with anticipation for him to get to work. I could not wait to see his large fifty cent looking eyes and his gorge smile as he walked through the back door of that kitchen. Without warning he was beginning to appeal to me.

Having no relationship and no one else to talk with, images of him plagued my mind. He was short, dark in complexion, very muscular, handsome, and pretty to the eyes; working two jobs, but much too young for me. I was nearly ten years older than him. And, he was nine years older than my oldest child. Therefore, this was a forbidden relationship.

However, as time goes bye, we began looking forward to seeing each other. When we saw each other we greeted one another with a smile. Our conversation would oftentimes started with joking, laughing and playing around. When we were not at working we would spend time together riding around town for hours.

This continued until one day we found ourselves locked armed in arms with each others. I had become mesmerized by his charming spirit. My flesh went mad lusting for him. I tried resisting him, but could not help my self. It was as though fate would not have it any other way. I had to feed my flesh, satisfying my sexual desires with this man. I knew I would be sinning against God, but for some unknown reason, it did not matter; I had to have him.

Then one day the inevitable happened, it was the start of an intense love affair. We were like two animals in heat, waiting to crawl between the sheets.

Dona' charming nature sparkled flames of passion within me. He had a way of standing behind me, gently allowing his body to brush against mind. As he stood there softly kissing my neck, he would cause me to nearly pass out from all of the excitement he ignited within me. Slowly pivoting his body towards the front of

Lord, Why Me?

mind, with one hand unhooking my bra, he directed me towards the bed where we would make love into the morning light.

Having a sexual encounter with him was an easy task for me. To be completely honest, this was the first time in my sex life; that I felt free to explore. Unlike other relationships, I was not afraid to touch him, to kiss him, to make love to him. I was awakened to sexual desires that I did not know existed.

Making love to this man was a pleasure even at the expense of losing my soul and going straight to hell. How foolish could I have been? No one had ever managed to excite me sexually as he had done.

Cohabitation was easy too. It gave us a true reason for sinning against God. The excitement of this sin, the desire and flame of passion that was awaken within my body told me it was alright to make love to this man as I was doing. He felt like my soul mate and I could not brush him off. I was infatuated with him.

Something was different about this man. When I looked into his eyes, it was as though I could see his heart. I could see that he was not lusting after me, but was indeed in love with me. No one had ever loved me for me, nor had I learned how to love myself. No one had ever romanced me as he had done.

He was the most generous and attentive man I had ever met. He was forever showering me with numerous gifts and cards. We were always going on some type of trip. He lavished me with many vacations. We would spend our weekends away from home staying at five star hotels, eating at the best restaurants. This continued for six years, at which time we decided to do the right thing.

We were in love and excited about each other or were we infatuated with each other? Finally, I was given the opportunity of meeting his family. I even meet his out of -town relatives and to my surprise they all approved of me. I took him home to meet my folks; they liked him although they thought he was strange.

Dona' Trust did everything in his power to make me happy and in return I turned into a spoiled brat. I did not ask him to buy things for me, all I had to do was mention what I wanted and before long, he gave it to me.

When Dona' Trust saw that I was becoming unhappy, he suggested I find something that would occupy my time and recommended I return to school. I was surprise that he would encourage me to do such a thing, however; I took his advice and began focusing my attention on getting even with the people that had hurt and left me.

Dona' told me that I could get revenge by finishing college. He said he would not become insecure nor bent out of shape when I finished my course because I was an asset and we were going to be together forever. With that thought in mind and the desire for revenge this became a driving force in my heart. I applied at a nearby university and was accepted.

As I aspired to obtain this Bachelor of Health Services Degree, I became weary and wanted to quit. But Dona' would not hear of it. He whispered in my ear how beautiful I was as a person and encouraged me to press on and to reach for the stars. He said he saw something in me.

With such encouraging words, not only did I graduate receiving a Bachelor Degree from Florida Atlantic University, I applied at a Catholic University for higher education in NW Miami. To my surprise, I was accepted into their graduate program, and a year later, I received a Master of Health Management Degree from St. Thomas University.

Three years go by and I have successfully accomplished my educational endeavors. During this time, it never dawned on me that I had not been employed, but had played the fatuous role of a house wife.

Dona' worked two jobs to support me and my four children, as well as his two. He contributed funds toward my college tuition and purchased a home for us. He bought me a new Cadillac so

Lord, Why Me?

that I would have transportation to and from school. He bought my first computer so that I would have no problems completing my college assignments. Financially, he was a life saver. No one had ever taken care of me like Dona' Trust, and I enjoyed every moment of being pampered.

Prior to shacking up with him and looking back, I can now say that I took his kindness for love, his warm smile told me he liked me, and his kind words thrust me into a passionate sexual rendezvous with him.

Graduation day came and Dona' Trust asked me to marry him. At first I said no, but after a while, I had a change of heart. I thought about all the things he had done for me. I believed he loved me and only me. Something in my heart told me that he was my soul mate and he would always be there for me.

After pondering over his question for a few days, I said "yes." I was at work when I called him telling him of my decision to marry him.

Shortly afterward, he showed up at my job with a great big smile on his face. He had a habit of showing up at my place of employment without calling. I never knew when he might pop up, so I was never surprised to see him.

On this particular day when he stopped by my place of employment as he usually did, he asked me to come outside. Taking his hand, he gently placed them over my eyes, leading me outside the back door of my office. He instructed me to keep my eyes closed until he said to open them. When he removed his hand, and I opened my eyes, I nearly fell over for dead upon seeing a brand new wine colored Lincoln Town car. This was my wedding gift for accepting his invitation of marriage. I loved the things he was doing for me, and because of his generosity towards me, this made him even more irresistible.

He was nothing like the other men whom I had been involved with. He was such an introverted person, the complete opposite of my self, who was an extrovert. He had a sneaky way about him and I was intrigued by this.

There was something different about him or so I thought, only to learn that this marriage like the others would be much more challenging. We told our children, loved ones, friends and family member about our decision to get married. My children did not like the idea of me getting married to him or anyone else. They wanted me back me with their father, but he had moved on with life and was married to his lover with whom he had a child. They were a family and I had no intention of wrecking their home. However, as time go by, and I explain things to them, they accepted the idea. Having their approval and being excited, we began planning for our wedding day. We began saving the necessary funds for this occasion, we looked at the wedding attire; we asked friends and family members to participate and during the following year we were married. Our honeymoon was spent in the Bahamas.

However; after two weeks into the marriage and nine months after completing my master's degree, I was offered a position as a Nursing Home Administrator with a small organization out of Mississippi.

This position would mean relocating. I was ecstatic about this offer. But I had a problem I was a newly wed and would need to consult my husband. After talking things over with him, him meeting my new bosses and after much consideration, we both agreed to this offer with the exception that he would relocate. My new bosses promised Dona' Trust a position in one of their facilities as a nursing home administrator as soon as an opening came about.

Dona' had completed his schooling with my help and was already employed as an administrator. My bosses saw this as an excellent opportunity for the two of us.

This was one of the happiest moments of my life and I guessed my husband knew that this move would mean an opportunity for career growth for me, especially since we both were employed in the same line of work.

Dona' Trust immediately began to assist me in preparing for my new endeavors. In doing so, he promised that he would move as soon as an opening came about. He was very attentive in helping me find a safe place to live. He assisted me in packing my belongings; rented a large moving truck, and he took me away.

I waited with anticipation on the day that he would arrive and we would finally be as one. However, it appeared that he was not going to move, but had tricked me into taking the position away from home.

Greenville, Florida was a very small town, so small until I was sure that everyone knew each other. On my first day at work, I was greeted warmly by the people of this town.

The staff was friendly and anxious to meet their new owners. And it did not take long for Satan to attack me.

Approximately three months after coming to Greenville, I found myself being tracked down like a rabbit being chased by a hound dog. The local newspaper reporters of that community wrote an article about the facility that had a negative connation to it. What they wrote was not good to the ears.

They took a picture of me and plastered it on the front page of their newspaper. I nearly died when I saw my face. To comfort my fears, I immediately took flight to West Palm Beach; where my husband resided. Little did I know that this negative publicity would cause me to receive a promotion with a larger company. In other words, what the devil meant for my harm, God turned it around for my good. Psalms 75:6 -7 declares:

> **For promotion cometh neither from the east, nor from the west, nor from the south. But God is the judge: he**

putteth down one, and setteth up another (NIV).

My bosses offered Dona' Trust a job at a nearby facility, as they had promised during our interview together, but he did not respond to their offer. The pay was great and he had no excuse for not taking this position, other than "He was not going to put all of his eggs in one basket." I could not believe that he had agreed to the move and agreed to accept a position with this organization, taken me away, then not accept the offer. I had moved to Tallahassee, Florida; the other end of the world. He lived in West Palm Beach and therefore I could not understand his reasoning for not accepting the position, nor relocating.

Everyday Dona' Trust called me like clock work and as always, I ended our conversation by asking him "When are you coming?" I never really got a response, but what I noticed was him evading the question.

My eyes were slowly opening as were my ears, to truth and it hurt. At first, I was in denial, I just did not want to believe that he had packaged my belongings, agreed to the move, shipped me away and now he was fabricating about relocating. Suddenly, the pieces of the puzzle started to fit and I did not like the way they were forming. This puzzle was ugly and had a taste of lies to its shape. My thoughts crashed harshly into the cells of my brain and I was not able to control them.

Upon realizing that he had not been totally honest with me, I became upset and relived childhood memories of abandonment and rejection, and without warning both panic and fear over took me. Every night I would wake up at three forty five in the morning. This was the time of the last rape. I became frighten of the night. I could see the face of the last man that raped me, him beating me unconscious, moving me from my bed to the bedroom of my mother. Memories that were suppressed came alive. My mind made me believe that people who had abused me were resurfacing.

After being on the job a month, as a Nursing Home Administrator the facility had become a mess. I started having chest pains and daily lost of vision due to stress. I was stressed over two things, Dona' Trust and my job. My first week at work, I was instructed to make cuts in the number of staff that we had. Overtime had to be cut out, staffing hours were changed in all departments, new policies and procedures had to be written and implemented, upsetting the staff, residents and family members beyond one's wildest imagination. And with all of this, I had to face facts, Dona Trust had lied to me and my new bosses about moving; both took its toll on my health.

The disappointment of realizing that this man was not going to move and finding out seven years into the marriage, he had fathered a child during the years we lived together, was a bit much for my mind.

Dona' Trust was not true to his word as I would later find out. He was just like Cheater John, but was far worse; he had fathered a child and had kept this child a secret all these years. The child would be seven years old when I made this discovery. Now it made sense why he would not move to Tallahassee. He was harboring secrets, secrets that would be determinant in the survival of our marriage.

He did not have morals enough to tell me about this child prior to asking me to marry him. When I discovered his unfaithfulness he outright denied this child. Dona' thought I was plain old stupid. The reality of being deceived again by someone I so deeply loved bought much pain and hurt to me.

This pain was so severe until I thought I would actually die. I could not understand how he could be so mean and cruel. How could he just take my love for granted; without regard to my feelings? How could he call telling me daily how much he loved me, yet treat my heart as though it was a piece of trash.

How could he let his heart out to play? And of course, how could I have been so foolish to have trusted him, when I had seen this type behavior before.

It would take me seven years after we were married to find out, all of his attentiveness and generosity was not as wonderful as he had made it appear. He had roaming eyes and not only did he have eyes that strayed, he was moody in personality, very secretive, fragile, and at times he could be brutally mean.

I came to understand that his attentiveness was just a camouflage to cover up his inability to be faithful. After scrutinizing him and seeing all that I saw, I was not at all happy with our living arrangements, but I was not about to walk away from this relationship. I needed somebody, plus I was in love with him. He became the crutch that I so very much needed and I was not about to throw them down.

Dona' Trust told me daily that he loved me, yet he had committed the unthinkable. This was crazy love and I guess he told me what I wanted to hear.

I found myself right back where I started from. I wanted to run away from this awful situation. I just didn't understand. My morals would not allow me to be dishonest in this relationship just as it would not with my past, maybe this was the punishment that God had given me for going against His Word, "Thou shalt not commit adultery."

As I rationalized my sins, I say to myself; I should have waited until Cheater John and I were divorced before I started sleeping with Dona Trust, but instead of controlling my flesh, I immediately started shacking up with this man.

I knew what the Word of God said, but nevertheless I was willing to sin against God, but was not willing to cheat on Dona'. I say to myself, "What's wrong with this picture?" "Have you completely lost your mind?" What I discovered was when sin is committed it is pleasurable and the end result is always death.

Realizing that I married a man with a lying spirit, and a heart that was not hesitant about cheating, I decided on nurturing myself. Taking care of my needs would be a hard task, but it was something that had to be done. During the past, I had never thought about taking care of me. I needed to learn how to love myself and if no one else loved me, I concluded, that would be alright too.

In an effort to forget my pain, I threw myself into making a success of my career, as well as improving my personal imagine. I started exercising daily and trusting God more. But to no avail could I not forget Dona' Trust.

In taking care of my self, the first thing I did was give my life completely over to the Lord. I came to understand that everything that I had accomplished was done through the power of God. I slowly allowed the Lord to show me truth and I was beginning to understand the scripture in John 8:32 which read:

"And you shall know the truth, and
the truth shall make you free."

Prior to this, I was merely like everyone else who declared they knew God. Yes, He answered my prayers and did strive with me, but did I indeed have a genuine relationship with Him?

When I became serious about God, things changed in my life. I made an effort to attend church on a regular basis, evaluating church folk: I noticed something about them that was most disturbing; they could be the meanest and most nastiest people one could ever encounter. Many of them did not extend a warm hand of welcome to new comers; instead they brush them off, ridiculing and talking harshly to potential members. Witnessing their behavior, I purposed in my heart to serve God with all my being.

I found myself not wanting to be just a "church go'er," someone who served God with my lips, and not my heart. I did not like what I saw in these so call Christians. Many of them pretending to love God: having *"a zeal of God but not according to the knowledge of God" (Romans 10:2, NIV)*. Some were acting as though they were Christians and maybe they were, but they surely were not "Practicing Christians."

The devil was using many of these church goers and I did not want to be like any of them. I began praying in an effort to develop a genuine relationship with God. I wanted to live aright before both God and man.

I became a Christian and was slowly transformed. My mind was changing as was my attitude. I did everything in my power to live according to the Word of God. God began revealing Himself to me. I saw that I could trust Him.

I wanted to do those things that was right and pleasing in his sight. God was blessing me and I was reaping the benefit of serving Him, although my personal life was in turmoil.

Several years passed and I had become known as a seasoned nursing home administrator. I had proven to the industry that I was capable of handling the day to day operation of their facility.

As time went by, several of the larger organizations tried recruiting me, but I was not moved by their recruitment package. I had one particular company in mind that I wanted to become employed with and that was the largest nursing home organization in the United States. But I understood how the business world worked. It was not what you knew that got you hired, but was who you knew that counted. With that in mind, I purpose in my heart to make my name known throughout the industry as an effective administrator.

I attributed my success as an Administrator from having an intimate relationship with God, and placing Him first in all of my decisions. I would not take a position unless I believed God had sent me to that facility. I also believed that my new bosses played a significant role in my success too. My boss had a way of making you think. If you asked him a question, he would lecture you before answering, opening your mind to the world of business.

I realized that my knowledge of long term care came from being employed by him and his wife. This position, (as was the case of my life,) would be one with many challenges, much more than I would envision, but overall my bosses were wonderful people.

I was eighteen months into my career, when I was offered a position with the largest nursing home chain in the United States.

One day while at work, my secretary buzzed my office informing me that the President of the largest nursing home chain in the United States was on the phone. I became nervous and could not understand why this man was calling me. I did not work for him, but was employed by a much smaller organization.

This man was a highly respected official in the industry. As far as I was concerned he was the kind of boss that anyone would love to work for. He could be firm but at the same time I found him to be fair and understanding. His reputation preceded him.

He was calling to offer me a position with his organization. This facility was located in Green Cove Springs, Florida.

It would mean leaving Tallahassee, Florida. A move I longed for every day. I dreaded seeing so many trees overlapping one another. It was as though I was living in the country. I just could not make the adjustments of moving from beautiful West Palm Beach, to the woody area of Tallahassee, it was a real culture shock for me.

Personally speaking, I was flattered to be receiving a call from Mr. Scotch Tell. [At first I found myself somewhat intimidated by this man of status; however, as we casually talked, my fears slowly diminished.] He started the conversation by asking about me. He then preceded by asking, "If I was happy working for my present employee? I responded by saying "yes." The next question he asked was "If I liked the idea of coming aboard his organization?" My response to this question was "yes, I would love that."

'May I schedule an interview?" he asked. I answered by saying "yes you may."

I immediately called Dona' Trust who eagerly meet me at a hotel in Orlando. I left work around six that evening so that I could make my appointment on time. Arriving, about twelve thirty in the morning, I was greeted by their Human Resources Director, Mr. Albert Sailor, who directed me to my hotel room. This man informed me that I would be meeting with six men from their organization on the next day.

At first I was petrified, but found the strength to calm myself when I thought of the long lectures that my former boss had given me. I told myself, "These guys were nothing in comparison to him.' Not even their intellectual level could be compared to my previous boss."

I meet with each of them around ten the next morning. Answering their questions and feeling good about the interview, I was again offered the position. After accepting the position, we agreed on an annually salary.

When I heard the amount I nearly screamed with joy. I thought I was hearing things. I wanted to jump up and shout "Thank You Jesus!" But I composed myself and waited until I hit the parking lot. I leaped in the air, grabbed Dona' Trust around the neck and praised God! We rejoiced together.

As I made my way back to Tallahassee, I called my friend Linda Blackshear Smith to break the news to her. She was happy for me. I knew I would miss her because she had been the only friend that I had while residing in Tallahassee. As a matter of fact, it was a pleasure meeting her because we had a lot in common. Her sister lived in the same hometown that I came from. She operated a small daycare center where many of the local children attended and had done so for years.

Making the long drive back home I pondered over how I was going to break the news to my bosses. Overall, they were wonderful people and in a way I hated leaving them. But there came a time when all good things must come to an end.

A month later, I found myself employed in the city of Green Cove Spring, Florida. This town was located near Jacksonville. I was extremely glad to be there, it was much closer to where my husband lived.

In my mind, it was back to city living, lots of people, places to go and things to see and do. I said to myself, this area is so much prettier than Tallahassee. A person can do much more here. With those things in mind, I was certain Dona' was going to relocate.

Dona' Trust and I decided to build our first dream home, and as always he was right there assisting me. He picked out the lot in which the house was to be built on, chose the colors for the inside and outside of the house. He selected the type of flooring and promised he was going to move this time. When our home was completed, I was eternally grateful to God. I was reaping some of the benefits of serving Him. He had blessed me with a decent income and with such a nice house, to the point where I was living "the life of Riley" as my grandmother would say. Several months later, I moved into our new home.

I started discarding all of the old furniture. Dona' Trust was not at all pleased with this decision, but nevertheless, I got rid of it anyway. He believed this furniture had sentimental value, but my views were not the same. It was furniture he had purchased when we were dating and for our new home, I wanted quality furniture. Furniture that would last as long as I lived.

When I finally settled into our new home, it was beautiful. We had more rooms that I ever dreamed of. We had moved up in the world. This house consisted of four bedrooms and two baths. A spacious kitchen, formal living and dining room, a large family room, two walk in closets in the master's bedroom having a huge bathroom with a Roman marble tube in the bathroom, "his and hers sinks: marble counter tops in both bathrooms, but no husband to share my dreams with.

As my career continued to flourish, so did my income, it exceeded my wildest dreams. I was ever so proud of my accomplishments. I was not doing bad for an old country girl who grew up in a small town called Hobe Sound, Florida. For the first time in history, I was able to live the kind of life that I had always dreamed of.

Dona' Trust once again promised to move with me, but he never showed up. Feelings of frustration overwhelmed me. And again, I rehearsed the past, examining it for clarification.

Throughout the industry I became known as a very good administrator. God had given me favor in operating a long term care facility. I repeatedly leaned on God for wisdom and direction.

As a result, destiny would carry me to many sick people. Not only did I have "Administrative" authority over the elderly, but God had given me "Spiritual Authority" as well. There were those family members who called upon me for spiritual advice. Often times I would be called from my office to pray for a dying loved one. It was not un-common for other administrators to call asking me to pray concerning the many issues we each faced as professionals. My staff saw the Spirit of God operating within me and when they did, I found myself praying and ministering to many of them.

In one particular community, I became known as the praying administrator; and in being recognized as this, I received several invitations to appear on church programs as their guest speaker.

Not only was I known for my strong faith in God to the community and staff I managed, my bosses saw the call of God in my life. Seeing that I was different than the other administrators, the "big wigs" (upper management) thought I was somewhat fruity because of my unshakable faith in God.

At one point, I was called to my boss office because several of the associates decided they did not like me and wanted me fired: just as they had done to the other administrators. They outright lied on me. I felt like Daniel, who was placed in the loins den and called before the king for refusing to obey his decree.

After talking with my boss and explaining what I was up against in the natural as well as the spiritual, he told me to go back to the facility and continue to pray. Strongholds were running rampant throughout the facility. It was as though I had entered the house of Satan. Staff was stealing, lying, selling drugs, sleeping with the opposite sex, whoring about and threatening every administrator that was hired. I was no exception. Satan wanted me out of this facility. He knew that God was building my character and my faith in Him.

I was questioned for expressing my faith in God to those that questioned me on what I believed. However, I stood firm on my belief in God. I refused to bow down and as a result of my standing firm, those that I came in contact with me, left knowing that I indeed had a relationship with a higher source, God that is.

I did not try hiding the fact that I was a Christian. How could I even attempt to go in to the campground of the enemy, if I did not have God on my side? I needed God if I were to be successful. I relied on Him to direct my footsteps: I needed the Lord to lead me in making decisions pertinent to those that I was in charge of. Everyday was like going on a battlefield. I found myself being attacked on every end. With much praying and fasting I was able to overcome, but not without a struggle.

During this time, I longed for Dona. I was all alone in a world by myself. No family, no friends and no husband, just a piece of paper saying I was married.

Examining my life, I could find no answers: no happiness anywhere; and there was a void in my life. I was lonely, upset and becoming bitter over this man's inexcusable behavior. However, I could not make myself leave him.

I loved him, he was the center of my life and for his love I would climb the highest mountain: swim the deepest sea, travel miles by feet, just to spend an hour with him. But his feelings were not mutual. He was distant, just as the miles between us that separated us, among other things.

My heart went out to God when I could find no peace. I cried out to God like I never had done before. I prayed day in and day out. This man had forced me into serving God wholeheartedly. Serving God was my only source of relief from the misery I lived. My heart became less troubled as I lifted my voice unto God. In my distress, I took refuge in the arms of Jesus. All those years that my aunt had prayed for me was now being answered. I was entering an intimate relationship with the Lord.

My desire was to be more like Jesus. Even in the mist of confusion, I could feel the presence of God all around me. I wanted to find means of discharging the stress that was in my life, so I enrolled in a Seminary School and obtained a Masters Degree in Ministerial Studies.

I became so intrigued in learning about God, until I felt compelled to stay another year, obtaining a Doctorate of Theology Degree from Truth Bible College and Seminary.

With all these degrees and in all of my accomplishments, I had not learned to successfully master and maintain a relationship.

Had my past cause me to be a failure in reaching true love, I asked myself? Was I not behaving as a good wife?

Didn't Dona' understand how important he was to me?

Why did he put me through school and now want to leave the relationship? Did he really want out of the marriage?

These were questions that I asked myself.

Something inside of me made me believed Dona' would soon relocated, but after numerous promises I had to accept truth in realizing that he was not going to leave his old hometown. So I cried out to God for strength to go on with my life and to accept those

things that I could not change. In crying out to God, I was falling in love with Him.
"I tasted the Lord and found him to be good." (Psalm 34:8, NIV). In serving Him I found much comfort and solitude. I knew that things would work out on my behalf, if I could just be patient: I just did not know when or how they were going to come about, but, I knew what the Word of God declared, and I believed everything that was written in the word.

With my heart wounded and spirit broken and with no where to turn I ran straight into the arms of Jesus. As I ran to Him, I could hear Him say to me:
> ***Let not your heart be troubled.***
> ***John 14: 1.***
> ***Come to me all you that are heavy***
> ***burden and cast thy burdens upon***
> ***the Lord.***

With years of serving Him and enjoying every moment of my relationship it enabled me to keep the hope that Dona' Trust would eventually move as he had promised repeatedly.

Life for me was forever changing. And with each change of season, and with every blessing, disappointment followed.

As I became a more seasoned administrator, and with every promotion, my income increased. As my income changed, so did my outlook on life. I understood the scripture which said, ***"God gives us the power to obtain wealth"*** *(Deut 8:18, NIV)*, and as a couple we were receiving money from every end.

Our small business had grown into a wealthy little company, accumulating asset well over one point two point five million dollars, according to his accountant. But with each goal accomplished, something disturbing was happening to our marriage.

Four years later, in the dawn of a hot summer morning, I received yet, another call from the same Human Resource Department: asking me to manage an even larger facility in Central Florida. I was extremely happy to be given this opportunity. It would definitely mean a tremendous pay increase and most of all; I was getting closer to home.

Living in this town for about a year, it became clear that I was not going back to Middleburg. I readily adapted to my new surroundings. I loved this place. For some unknown reason, I felt connected. I could feel the presence of God here.

In feeling His presence, I became comfortable in who I was, and, in what I was doing. After examining this city, and loving it much more than Middleburg, Dona' and I decided to sell our home and build another one in this new city.

Dona' instructed me to search out the city for land and to let him know what I found. I started my search and was totally blown away by my findings. I stumbled on land in an exclusive housing development in Orlando. The area was affordable and beautiful. I called Dona' the very same day notifying him of my findings.

Dona' made a visit to Orlando and agreed with me. Again, he went through the same ritual playing the role of a concerned husband. He had a habit of making sure I stayed in a safe environment. Dona talked with the developer and liked the price of the houses. When we finally found the house that we both wanted, he did as he had done with the first house. Identified the landsite: selected the model house, picked the colors scheme: designed the kitchen set up and flooring to his liking.

When this house was completed, it would be even larger and even more beautiful than the first. It would have five bedrooms and three full bath, a very spacious kitchen and of course, a formal living and dining room. In this particular house, it would include a playroom and a family room with a small porch where we could sit and watch the wonderful works of God.

I told myself, now, Dona' will not have any excuses for not moving with me this time. Orlando, will be close enough for him to travel back and forth to West Palm Beach, if need be.

I also said to myself maybe, "one day he will, leave his mother and cleave to me, his wife," as according to Matthew 19:5, (NIV). Like always this was not the case, my spirit man told me that he had no intentions of ever relocating.

I waited and hoped that Dona' would not have any more excuses for not moving. However, as like the other times, he provided me with some off the wall excuse as to when he would be moving. This time he gave me a date: which would be several months down the road, and I accept his schedule.

But something was really disturbing about his behavior, I was seeing less and less of him. My prince charming, my shy husband, had all of a sudden turned into a "night club hopper." He was hanging out with the guys and these boys had the reputation of being dope dealers and womanizers.

Instead of facing truth, I chose to close my eyes to reality, in hope that he is the husband; I desperately wanted him to be.

Who is this man? Why can he not get his act together? What would make him feel disconnected from our marriage? Was he trying to drive me insane with his craziness? These were the questions I asked myself.

My mind appeared to be going in circles, and feelings of rejection and disbelief were overshadowing me. I could not believe what I was hearing. I just would not allow myself to come to grip with truth. Something in my mind and heart would not allow me to come to term with reality.

My mind told me I was losing Dona' Trust to the streets, and to this mystery woman. What was I to do? He was deceiving me and I allowed him to do so because I was deceiving myself. The Bible declares in Proverbs 12: 20:

> *"Deceit is in the heart of them that imagine evil: but to the counselors of peace is joy."*

9

A SHATTERED HEART

It had been nearly seventeen years since Dona' Trust and I had been together. These were the most turbulent times of my life, especially after we were married. Years spend with this man consisted of much blood, sweat and tears. He had changed tremendously after our wedding vows. It was the most laborious relationship I had ever encountered. Living with Dona' Trust was like watching an action thriller combative movie. You never knew what he was going to do next. His behavior and attitude fluctuated between good and bad all the time. When he was good, you could not ask for a better person, but when he was bad, he could be Satan; himself.

I saw changes in his personality once we were married. However; they were silently unfolding as time progressed. My knight and shining armor had changed so much until he had become a stranger to me, one that managed to turn into a nightmare. In this dream, I was hearing what no wife wants to hear; voices echoes rumors of infidelity concerning him.

We had had our fair share of problems, but had some how managed to work through them. Many of our friends who were married during the time that we married, were long separated or divorced. But by the grace of God we were still together. I tried hard not accusing him of anything, especially when I felt jealous or insecure. But this time it would be extremely difficult not accusing him. Rumors were circulating around town about him having a three month old baby girl.

Prior to taking our nuptial vows, I made it plain and clear, I did not believe in having extramarital affairs and therefore; my level of tolerance was zero. I believed marriage is honorable and something that should not be taken for granted. It is a gift from God that He gave both man and woman so that they could show their commitment to one another. Most importantly, both husband and wife had taken an oath before God of their commitment to each other.

Marriage took the sin out of sex, which also was a gift from God. Sex was given to man and woman as a mean of satisfying their sexual desire of oneness as husband and wife. It is viewed as the coming together and possessiveness of two people in fulfilling and inward and outward yearning of love.

Sex was not given to a man to be used as a sport. It was never intended to defile the bed nor was it given to man or woman to be used in a casual manner. The scripture declares in I Corinthians 6:13:

> **"Now the body is not for**
> **fornication, but for the Lord;**
> **and the Lord for the body"**
> *(italics, NIV).*

In other words, sex without marriage is forbidden in the sight of God. Fornication should not be mistaken as adultery which has to do with unfaithfulness of a married person. God frowns on both fornication and adultery. As a matter of fact, God gave man a directive in Exodus 20:14 which read:

"Thou shalt not commit adultery." Adultery can also be defined as a sexual act between a married person and someone else other than the person spouse.

I in particular did not wish to go against God's Word and in keeping God's Word Holy; I did not want to give room to Satan when it came to our marriage. This was a serious covenant that I had taken before God and I was not about to violate it. I tried everything in my power to fulfill all of Dona's Trust sexual desires. I did not want him having any excuses for having an extramarital affair. And although our marriage was a "commuter marriage," I made every effort of getting home so that we could get between those sheets.

However, after coming into the knowledge of God, studying His Word, receiving understanding of the Word; I came to learn that if a man or woman has a lust spirit, their sex desire can not be fulfilled by any one person. This desire could be so strong until they themselves would always be seeking sexual pleasure outside of the marriage, therefore they can never fulfill that part of their life. They must received deliverance from God to abstain from sexual immorality.

Lust is like an appetite, it must be fed and cannot be satisfied with a substitute. It is a strong overwhelming desire that searches for fulfillment in ways not acceptable unto God. Therefore; a person acquiring a strong sex desire will stray outside of the covenant of marriage, without regard to the oath taken before God.

Lust will cause a person to secure those things which may or may not be good for them. It motivates an individual to long for or to move towards that thing which it yearns for. Henceforth, man when he is unfaithful to God, he will be lustful. Lustfulness breeds unfaithfulness and unfaithfulness will lead man towards deceitfulness and deceitfulness will breed infidelity. Infidelity therefore produces adultery in marriage and causes scandalous sin disgracing the covenant of marriage before God and man.

Dona' Trust eyes said that he was lustful, something I had not seen until it was too late. I noticed him watching women rear ends as they walked pass him. He did it in such a sneaky way, dropping his head then slowly looking up at her butt. He also had a playful way with people of the opposite sex. His charming mannerism having a flirtation overtone told me that there was a spirit of lust lurking within him. These would be the things that created unnecessary problems in our relationship. He was like a mischievous child, always getting into something.

He could not accuse me of not performing my duties as his wife. I had no problems about cleaning, because I am a "neat freak." I had no trouble with cooking, because I love "making my man fat." I had no difficulties with washing nor ironing because this is a part of good housekeeping, and I most certainly did not have qualms about fulfilling his sexual desires. I was a lady in the living room, a woman in the kitchen and his private dancer in the bedroom. My goal was to keep him happy. I was not one of those women that said "no," nor did I have headaches because I found sex to be a remedy for that problem. My suggestion to him was "tell me how you like it baby."

However, I did have one real problem and that was, I could get very, very, wacky if you played with my emotions. He would need to sleep with one eye opened and the other closed or he might need to place a clothes hanger on the bedroom door just to get a good night sleep and to know my whereabouts.

In other words, commitment is one of the most important aspect for building a lasting relationship. Without it, trust and communication there will be absolutely no chance of relationship survival. My philosophy was, if you did not have trust, commitment and communication you could not build a solid relationship. What is a relationship without all three? In a simple answer, nothing!

Dona' and I were invited to Blackshear, Georgia with a friend and his family. This would be a great and needed chance for the two of us to rekindle our love. It would mean him getting away from the hustle and bustle of city life. We had a wonderful time. He was relaxed, humble, friendly, smiling and enjoying life for a change. Relaxing to the point where all of us were picking Asian apples. Whenever we went out of town, he could let his guard down and enjoy life for a moment. But the minute we hit the Florida

State line, he would become nervous as though he had something to hide. He would become tensed and on the edge. During our three day vacation, he made small talk with the people we were visiting, but he mainly sat around observing everyone as he had always done. He was never much of a talker. During the eighteen and a half years that we were together he did not ever say much. If said he spoke a years worth of words, I was lucky.

Several days after returning home from Blackshear, I received a call from Sherry. She said to me, "Nana, my sister's husband has been having an affair and has a three month old baby girl." What would you do if that was Dona Trust?

Stunned by her question, I took a deep breath and asked, "Sherry what are you trying to tell me?' She responded by saying, "Nana, Dona' has been having an affair and he has a three month old baby girl.' He has been cheating on you and his girlfriend has been coming around my job everyday showing off her baby." "She even gave me her phone number, do you want it?" I answered "yes."

I called the number and Dona' Trust girlfriend answered. I asked politely to please speak with Imma Home Wrecker, when she responded, I identified myself as Mrs. Dona' Trust. I could tell from the nervousness of her voice and the gashing for air as we briefly talked that it was her. When she identified herself, I asked her a series of questions. However, she flat out denied being involved with my husband and denied having a baby by him. I asked her, "Why would you put out a rumor that you have a baby by my husband if it was not true?" She became extremely nervous and hung up the phone.

Something on the inside of me told me that she was lying and I should probe just a little bite further. I called Dona' and could tell from his trembling voice that Imma had called him notifying him that I knew about the two of them. I asked him, "Who is Imma and what is she to you?"

His response was, "I don't know no Imma." I said to him, "yes you do, she is the female that has a baby from you." He flat out denied knowing her and having a child by her, just as he had done the first child thirteen years ago.

I responded by telling him that, "I was going to God in prayer and I was going to tell Him how he had treated me. I also told him that I was going to ask God to reveal truth to me and to make all of his secrets known. And when He showed me truth, to please set me free.

I was in bondage, bondage to confusion, bondage to his lies that he constantly told to cover his tracks, bondage to betrayal, bondage to bitterness, angriness and resentment.

And I wanted to be free. He then hung up the phone.

As I rehearsed life history with Dona' I was slowly realizing I had allowed this man to play me for a fool.

A fool that had been mistreated by the man she loved. By showing me love through material things. He lavished me with gifts, expensive vacations, cars, houses and jewelry.

As a fool I no longer wanted to play the role of "wait and see." I had waited with the first child and it would be seven years into our marriage when I discovered her existent, so I was surely not going to wait eighteen years more to find out truth about this ghost of a baby.

I wanted to face my fears, hurt, disappointments and disbelief so that I could make decisions pertinent to my future. Dona' tried convincing me that the rumor was not true and that Imma was angry at him for refusing to rent her one of our houses. He said, "He had never been unfaithful to me during the entire time we had been married, I only thought about it, but I did not do it." He looked me in the eyes, swearing to God that he had never been unfaithful to me. I did not believe him. I had seen him cry too many times when he had gotten in trouble in our marriage, so I was not buying that. My female intuition told me he was lying and was indeed having an extramarital affair.

I revisited the first incident with the first child. I thought about the time when I found papers showing he had bought a house with a female co-worker, this legal document said he was a single male. I mediated on the times when my girlfriend told me that she saw him leaving the hotel with a female and she also saw him another time having early morning breakfast with another female. My mind went back to when he accidentally told me about two female tenants who were fighting over him and the police had to be called to break them up. With this incident, I was sure he was having an affair. Females only fight over a man when he has been intimate with her. She is much like a cat, she "pisses" on her spot and always goes back to smell it. I thought about the reprimand that I found from his job concerning him and a female employee. I could not help but think about the condoms that I found under the seat of his car and in his dresser draw, hid beneath his socks and underwear.

When I approached him about the condoms, he claimed he had been given them by the Health Department when they were passing them out. I later found out, Imma Home Wrecker mother was employed at the Health Department. I refused to believe anymore of his lies. He thought I was stupid and that I was so in love with him that I would allow him to treat me like some slut in the street.

Soon real evident of cheating was beginning to surface.

Imma Home Wrecker began showing up in places where she knew the news would get back to me. She started riding on the street where we lived; however, at the time, I did not know who she was. I recognized her once I meet her face to face. Dona' kept on lying about not being involved with anyone. And I keep on praying asking God to help me through that awful situation.

I was trying to live a Godly life. I wanted to do things that were right by God, my husband and man. The more I prayed the harder Satan kept coming up against me. He was attacking every aspect of my life and my home front was the most burdensome challenge of them all. As I prayed I could discern numerous spirits all around me. A spirit of lies, a spirit of betrayal, a spirit of confusion, a spirit of adultery, rejection, bitterness, jealousy, resentment and division.

During one church service that we were attending, God told both Dona and I that a spirit of division had been sent against me and that it was sent to make me turn away from God. God said that this spirit was targeting our marriage and for Dona' to come clean and for me to "stand still."

I became angry and cried out to God. Lord! Why Me?

Why must I go through so much? Why must I have to deal with this man when I know that he has cheated on me?

Why had I have to endure so much pain? Afterward, I repented for asking so many questions and asked God to give me the strength to hold on.

Imma Home Wrecker was getting bolder and bolder, she wanted my husband and would do whatever it took to get him. She did not seem bothered by the facts that lots of innocent people would be hurt by both her actions and Dona's. She began flashing her baby picture all around town hoping someone would tell me. The more she flashed, the more Dona lied.

I could no longer take the lies and feared Dona would force me to snap, I went back to Central Florida, my home away from all of the craziness surrounding him.

As I made my way back home, I cried out to God for directions. I needed to determine where I was going with all of this unexpected news. I asked myself, "how could Dona make the same mistake twice in a row, thirteen years later?'

It was clear to me that he did not love me nor did he have respect for me as his wife.

Days go by and I was home seeking God for truth and clarity. I had resigned to the fact that our marriage was over but, Dona' refused to leave me alone. He started calling back to back, non-stop. When I refused to answer the house phone he would call my cell phone. I politely called the cell phone company and asked them to change my number.

I must have changed my number ten times and each time I changed the number, he got the number before I could even remember my new phone number. I was annoyed at his behavior and was becoming even more resentful of the fact that he would treat me so bad then call me a thousand times.

His calls were persistent and he refused to give in until I answered. When I answered the phone, he tried convincing me how much he loved me by saying "he would love me always and forever." He tried telling me "that no other woman could ever take my place no matter how she tried." However, I was too hurt to hear him. I had heard all of those lies before.

This time he told me that he would move to Orlando and I believed him. I believed if he moved and we were under one roof as husband and wife we could put the past behind us and move towards the future. Something on the inside of me said, "how could you move towards the future when he's not being honest?' 'How could we, if he was telling me what I wanted to hear?" Trying to sooth things and to fool me, he came to Orlando for a few days. I could feel the presence of the other woman and I knew once he was headed back to West Palm Beach, he was going to kill himself calling Imma. She was like a ghost lurking about our home.

Her presence made me stay on my knees before God. I knew that God knew exactly what the both of them were doing and I understood the Word of God when it declared, **"there are no secrets under the heavens that shall not be revealed."** So I had to trust God in showing me Dona's deceitful heart.

Dona and I tried talking, but he had a habit of evading certain questions. I wanted truth and was not about to let my suspicious go away. He seemed scared and distant, lost in space and worried half to death. I wanted to know the truth.

I prayed and I prayed asking God to help me. I asked God to give me strength to hold on and to help me not turn away from Him because of all the trials I had to endure.

A small still voice would awaken me during the night instructing me to "get up and go out to Dona's truck and look under the seat. This voice told me to check his cell phone bills, check book and receipts. I would get up following instructions to the letter. Each time I would find something that said he was not being honest.

Finally, this voice would eventually lead me to Imma Home Wrecker. She was working at a nearby thrift shop when I meet her. I did not approach her, but Kesia did and when she did she asked if I would get out of the car and talk with her. As I walked up to her, I was totally insulted by her posture.

Dona had decided to have an affair with someone he would eventually have to take care of. He had traded in an asset for a liability. We were nothing alike at all. We had absolutely nothing in common. The only thing that she had on me was the fact that she was twenty years younger than I, but I had her beat in every aspect of life. Dona had added insult on top of injury.

What was Dona' thinking about? Had his lustfulness completely overtaken him? Had he lost his mind? Was he looking for someone that he could control? I could not believe what I saw. This man had been so good to me. He had encouraged me, pushed me in to my destiny, helped me obtain four degrees. What was the problem? Our daughters were almost ready to leave home and it was our time to enjoy life, yet he had done the unthinkable and was trying to keep it hid. I had blossom into a beautiful rose and was learning to enjoy life even with our marriage being rocky.

I thought to myself, what is wrong with this girl, is she stupid? Why would any woman allow a man to make a secret of her? Why would she allow herself to be second in any man's life. Was her self-esteem that low?

Did she not have any self respect? Was she not ashamed of the sin that she had committed against God and herself? Did she not care that one day she would have to explain to her daughters the wrong that she had done in bringing them into the world? And finally, where was her self worth? Did she think so little of herself? Did she not care that her daughters might one day grow up and follow in her footsteps? I could not understand her, nor could I figure out how any woman could allow herself to get entangled in a situation such as this. Even if it was money, I would not stoop that low. I told myself, maybe the woman that is caught in this trapped is there because of her emotions, she is in the same situation as the battered woman, trapped and can not get out. She is being used, caught in a web of lies and trapped like a fly in a spider web.

Feeling betrayed, disappointed, resentful, bitter and angry, Dona was pushing me into a fit of rage. I had had it with him and wanted him to hurt just as I was hurting. I had never been unfaithful to him, because it was something that I did not believe in. However, my tongue could be much worse than cheating. It could be a lethal weapon, especially when pushed. I could be worst than a rattler snake, my victim once stroke would need medical attention immediately.

Maybe I should have bridle my tongue, but I could not. I had had enough. I was mad and this angry spirit brought with it a spirit of division and my tongue became a sword (rightfully dividing). I was determined to inflict pain upon Dona. I found myself moving away from God not wanting to wait on God to solve my problems. My patience had been worn out and I believed God needed some help. I had become bitter and angry over everything that I had endured throughout life. I did not want to wait on God, it appeared He was moving too slow and it had been nearly five years that I was troubled by Dona' atrocious behavior. I was tired and decided to take things in my own hands. In the end, I prayed for forgiveness.

Dona had worked my nerves, my cup had run over and I did not want to play with him anymore. I instructed him to "go" and just leave me alone, "go to your girlfriend," she deserved him, not I.

One day, while cleaning our home, Dona' Trust presented me with a large diamond ring valued at over eighteen hundred dollars. After examining this ring and becoming concerned, I was now certain he had done something wrong. When he gave me this gift, I said to him, "thank you, but what have you done? The bigger the gift, the greater the sin." To my surprise, his facial expression was that of shock. He looked as though he had seen a ghost.

Taking a deep breathe, looking about the room, he opened his mouth as though he was going to respond.

Dona's attitude had changed dramatically since we were married. I wondered if our small business had pushed him to the point of being out of control. When our income exceeded both our wildest imagination this is when he seemed to take a turn in the wrong direction. He was becoming popular, something he had not been prior to meeting me; so I was told. He was enjoying the attention that he was being showered with, especially from the women.

After going into real estate and purchasing many apartments and houses, his disposition changed beyond recognition. He was an expert at acquiring rental properties, although many of these places were in the "hood" (the ghetto that is). Our asset had moved from around sixty thousand a year to more than one point two five millions dollars. He bought everything under the sun: houses, cars, jewelry just to name a few. He was starting to feel like "Mr. Big Stuff."

His head was starting to swell. All of a sudden, he was visiting the local taverns; which had become a ritual. Prior to acquiring wealth he was much more humble and would have never spent time in a bar; this was the factor that drew me to him. However, he was changing for the worst and I could not understand this change. Rumors were circulating all around town about his sudden change in attitude and behavior.

I continued praying, but it seemed the more I prayed the worst things got. I fasted and I prayed, crying out to God for mercy, but these strongholds were getting stronger. It looked as though God had taken a vacation on me. My prayers, fasting and crying out to God seemed as though they were just going to the top of the ceiling and were bouncing back down hitting me in the top of my head. I decided again to take things into my own hands. My tired was tired and I had made up my mind to fight my own battle, God was taking a little too long.

At one point, Satan came to me telling me to just beat the crap out of Dona' Trust. I took a steel bat and told Dona, "I was going to knock the back of his head off if he continued to play with my emotions." I walked the streets of West Palm Beach until around one in the morning trying to find answers.

I was trying to hold on and do the right thing but Satan was using every fiery dart that he could against me. Dona' did not like me as a godly woman, he said, "he liked the old me. The old me would curse him from "A to Z" and think nothing of it. She would stand in a chair, light three cigarettes and blow smoke right dead in his face, yet he liked that person verses the woman that was trying to walk aright before God.

The old me would wait with anticipation for Friday to come so that she could get sweet revenge on him for some bad behavior he had displayed. She would disappear not returning until Monday evening after work. However, he told me that he liked me the old way. Was he as dysfunctional as I was?

I had made a conscientious effort to change. I wanted to change in such a way that God and man would be pleased. I vowed to live according to the Word of God even if I fell down a thousand times, I planned on getting up with a repentance heart.

Lord, Why Me?

I cried out to God in my despair, asking him to please help me. I asked repeatedly, "Lord, why me"? "Why must I go through so much with this man?" "What have I done to deserve this type treatment?" "Lord, Why me?'

The more I prayed: the worst things got. Finally on November 22, 2003, things took a toll for the worst between us. As Dona' and I were making love during the early morning hours as we had done during the past, the phone rung. Dona did not answer nor did I. We continued enjoying the bedroom pleasures of marriage. However, I noticed a slight change in the rhythm of his body. He seemed preoccupied and a bit nervous. I did not say a word, I got up, headed to the bathroom, cleaned up: made breakfast and did my wifely duties for the day.

I prayed as I had always done daily, read my Bible and tried to commune with God. All of a sudden, I heard a voice telling me "Get up and check the caller id." I obeyed the voice, went to our room and discovered that it had been unplugged. Strolling down the hall to the computer room, I checked that one too, finding Imma Home Wrecker number. I dialed her number and hung up, waiting on her to call back as I knew she would. Within a few minutes she called back, boldly asking for Dona' Trust.

Shortly afterward, Dona' rushed through the door in a state of panic, going straight to our room. When he ascertained I was talking with her, he snatched the phone from me, hanging it up.

We began fussing about his lack of respect for me. I was livid. A few minutes later she called back, talking to him. I was so upset over his behavior towards me until I became violent. I grabbed the hammer threatening to knock a hole in the top of his head. I leaped in the air, when I landed on my feet, striking the wall as hard as I could with my fist, putting him on notice that "he could not beat me that night."

Hurt, upset, frustrated and mad, I went back to our room and prayed. I got in bed and was reading my Bible when all of a sudden

I saw two policemen standing in our hallway. The officers asked, "Is there a problem here?" I replied, "No, we were just having an argument." The next thing I heard was Dona' Trust saying, "She hit me in the head with the hammer." The officer said, "Where is the blood if she hit you in your head with the hammer?" I said to the officer, "If I had hit that Negro in the head with the hammer, he would not be standing there talking to you."

The officers listened to both side and gave each of us an ultimatum, which was, one of us would have to leave our house that night or go to jail. Dona' Trust tried his best to have me arrested, stating "He was afraid of me and was scared to go to sleep because he thought I was going to hit him in the head with the hammer."

I told the officer that I was not going to hit him, but he was insisting that I leave. I packed my belongings and started walking towards my daughter's house.

As I walked towards my daughter's house, I dialed her cell phone in hope that she would be home so that she could come and get me. I could not believe that Dona' was trying to have me arrested. I thought to myself, "This is not fair. I have not done anything but loved this man and this is the thanks I would get."

I begged God to help me. I reminded Him of his word and told God how I had tried to live aright. I reminded God how I had obeyed his word and I was dependent upon Him: fighting my battle. After praying I heard a voice saying, "Go, I will be with you until the end."

I later learned that Imma Home Wrecker, his girlfriend called the police stating that I was going to kill Dona. She was on the phone as we were having our dispute and had taken it upon herself to bring closure to our marriage.

As I walked away, I visualized a funeral in process. The church was full of people. They were standing all around, some even lined the wall of the church. There was not an empty seat to be found. People were screaming, crying and were upset over this death. I slowly made my way to the front of the church: where the funeral director motioned for me. The minister spoke in a small soft voice. As I listened to him, he soon completed the eulogy, my mind rehashed our past. When he finished his sermon and the choir sang, "Bye and Bye oh when the morning Come," the Funeral Directors opened the casket for the last viewing. Everyone standing in the back of the church began making their way to the front in hope of paying their last respect to the deceased.

As I sit with my head dropped, the director slowly moved the casket closer to me so that I could bring closure to this event. To my dismay it's my marriage. The vows we had taken were deceased and had gone the last mile of the way and I could not believe it.

Finally, the funeral director and all of the pallbearers pushed this casket to the cemetery where a hole had been dug so that we could bury the corpse.

Imma wanted Dona' and she did not care how she got him nor did she care about the people whom she would hurt to get him. On several occasions she and I had our disputes over my husband, but I decided not to argue with her over him. She had no rights other than being "his baby mama." And I made up my mind that I was not wasting my time arguing with her over property that she had no rights too. I went straight after him. If any one was to blame the responsibility rested on his shoulder. Yes, she was a factor, but was not totally to blame.

Dona' had not behaved as a married man should have and had a problem with keeping his penis in his pants other than to urine. In a sense he was worst than Cheater John. And after examining his history with women, I noticed that he too would screw "women" from eight to eighty, black or white, fat or skinny, old or young. This was exactly what he had done. All of us were different in height, size, color looks, and he loved woman with "no booty."

The flatter the booty, the more he was intrigue with it. And there was me having a truck load and gun holsters for hips.

Living separate lives and having a commuter marriage had taken its toll on the both of us. I said to myself, 'if he had not been persistent in calling a thousand times per day, I would have left the marriage long ago."

How did we survive this long and why? What did God have in store for us or was I being tested? In evaluating our peers, I couldn't help noticing that everyone who was married during the year we were married were all divorced.

Our marriage had not been exempted from having its fair share of problems. Somehow we had always managed to work through our disagreements.

Prior to learning about this last incident, we decided to take another vacation, something we had not done for years. We went to Jamaica and had a blast. We were hoping to ignite flames and to rekindle our passion for each other. We had a wonderful time. I wished we did not have to return to the United States.

When he admitted he had been unfaithful, I wanted to have a pity party, but decided against it. To hear him admit to being sexual involved with another female crushed my tiny heart into a million little pieces. However, I picked up the pieces, brushed the shell rock fragments from my heart, and removed myself from the shock of actually hearing him admit to cheating: I said to myself, "Yes, I am out of here, I am free" as according to the Word of God.

I immediately rushed to my attorney's office, with money in hand that I had put aside for this occasion, but like a desperate man he refused to allow this marriage to be buried.

The number of times he called me was enough to make anyone in their right mind give in. He called me thirty five hundred times until I responded. I said to him "God is going to need to speak to me in order for me to stop this divorce." I was very adamant about this decision and refused to listen to anything anyone had to say. I did not want to hear what anyone thought, nor suggested concerning the decision I had made.

His daughters who were not my biological children, were devastated when they learned of their father's unfaithfulness. I raised both of them and treated them no different than I did my children. Dona acted as though they were the last thing on his mind. He had a "ready made family" and the interloper's children were calling him Daddy.

His oldest daughter handled the news of her dad very poorly. She became angry at him, refusing to accept either of her sisters. She would cry to me saying, "Mama I am never going to accept Daddy's mess." She refused to acknowledge Imma Home Wrecker at all. And at the time I did not encourage her to do that which was right because I was so upset over the entire situation and especially the manner in which Dona' was treating all of us.

Our baby girl was not bothered as much. She understood the definition of being mistreated and willingly accepted her sisters. As a matter of fact, she was extremely happy to learn that she had sisters, but was not pleased in the manner in which her father had going about things.

Therefore leaving both of his daughters no other choice but to find comfort and understanding from me. I tried explaining the situation to them as best I could, but in reality I was the wrong person for them to talk with. My feelings of the entire mess were reflecting in my answers and since I was hurting, I sometimes gave bad advice, yet I continued to pray.

I prayed when I was right and I prayed when I was dead wrong. I prayed about everything under the sun. I prayed good prayers and at times I prayed deadly prayers. God was answering every prayer that I prayed and was doing so in a hurry, all except the prayer concerning my marriage.

At last my prayers were answered, however not in the manner

in which I expected them to be. For years I cried out to God asking Him to show me what Dona' was hiding and to help me through this trial.

In praying I was hoping that Dona' Trust loved me enough not to betray or hurt me as he had done in the past. I wanted to believe that he had changed for the better. Deep down inside something kept telling me, he had not change and was only trying to fool me.

After talking with Dona' Trust, a small still voice said to me, "he's not sorry for what he has done, but is sorry that he's gotten caught." This voice told me that 'his behavior was not new and was something that he had been doing all along."

Hearing the voice of God made me take inventory of his past relationships. What I discovered brought chills over my body. Dona' had a habit of dating two women simultaneously. When I met him he was involved with Shirley and Barbara. When that relationship was over it was Beverly and I, then me and Imma Home Wrecker and God knows who else.

Over the years we had both changed. Could we have changed so much until we had taken each other for granted? Did my schooling cause me not to care? Or had he become insecure in knowing that I could now stand on my own? At one point in life we were such good friends: laughing, playing and joking with each other. We vowed to be friends forever and now the inevitable was here staring us boldly in our face.

Learning that Dona' had fathered another child was more than I could bear. I was angry and could not understand why each of us would invest so much in the relationship, then turn around and sabotage it.

In an effort to understand why both of us showed signs of being co-dependent, I focused all of my attention on his weakness not wanting to look at myself.

I wanted to blame him for this mess up. Deep down within I

felt I was the "perfect wife." But, who was I fooling? No one but; myself. Yet, I scrutinized him, looking for everything he had ever done wrong.

I had my fair share of problems, but not to the extent of cheating. I had a big mouth, but that should not have been a reason for him committing adultery. Or maybe I had treating him like a son verses a husband.

Was Dona' Trust having problems in identifying whom he was or was this his way of compensating for his in ability to become interlocked?

Was he mad or just plain crazy? How could he fall prey to a seducing spirit? Did he not realize that it was his persistent that enabled me to become the person that I have become? Didn't he understand that it was he who helped me grow up?

I had grown in more ways than one? I did not look the same. My way of thinking had changed as had my personality. Everything appeared to be in my favor except my marriage.

As for me, I had always known that my elevator did not reach the top floor. Maybe I should have bridle my tongue and done as the Bible instructed me and that is *"wives, submit yourselves unto your own husbands, as unto the Lord" (Ephesians 5:22, NIV).*

I could not scrutinize him only, I had to look at myself and this was not an easy task. I had my part in helping to destroy the relationship. I could be harsh, stiff-necked, high-strung and of course a little delirious if pushed.

Did we want to destroy the relationship or did we not know better? At times I believed both of us had worked hard at keeping the relationship alive and at other times we did everything to destroy it, we wanted out. However, each time we tried leaving each other, past memories would pull us back together.

One thing was clear; this relationship had consisted of alot of blood, sweat and tears. This was the most laborious relationship I had ever experienced. I say to myself, "I was tired. I could not hold on any longer." I was feeling as though I have had enough of the aggravation and just wanted a little peace of mind. I was tired of living on the edge, fearful of what might happen next. For years, I had to wrestle with all of his secrets, hiding things from others to keep from being ashamed. I had pretended to be happy when I was plain old disgusted with his behavior. I had no more strength nor did I not want to keep on deceiving myself and I did not want to continue verbally abusing him. I was mentally exhausted. I did not believe that God designed marriage to be like ours.

I was sick of sitting in his presence, listening to him talk on the phone with his girlfriend while I pretended to be preoccupied. I was living a lie. I knew each time his beeper went off in the middle of the night, a female was paging him. But I tried turning a deaf ear.

Dona' told me he loved me even while having an affair, maybe he did, but his love was not the kind that I deserved. I guess you could say; I was living in a fairytale world because I wanted a love that pure and honest. I was looking for a man that believed in commitment and not one who would intentionally inflict pain and sorrow upon the person whom he said he loved, all because of a roaming eye. Maybe I was asking too much, but I did not think so.

When all was said and done, I found myself asking the question, "Lord, Why Me? Why, must I endure so much pain, why so many tears?" God's response to me was, "I am the potter and you are the clay. In this plate there are many speckles that must be removed from your life. Trust me, what the enemy means for your bad, I shall turn it around for your good."

Finally, I was determined to leave the relationship, I had found reasons according to the Bible; but, like the first husband he just would not let go. I realized that I needed to move on because I was in a relationship with an unfaithful person, one who did not understand what the word commitment meant. I did not want any part of this; all I wanted was to heal and to move on with life. How could I heal if I continued to give in to him?

I cried out to God about my decision to divorce Dona' Trust. To make sure God understood what I meant, I reminded Him of His Word which says in Matthew 5:32, NIV:

> ***Whosoever shall put away his wife,***
> ***let him give her a divorcement...***
> ***that whosoever put away his wife,***
> ***saying for the cause of fornication***
> *(italics added).*

It was easier said than done, my mind floated back through time: making it an even more arduous task. I thought about our good days, our bad days; our loving moments, when we first met. I thought about our first kiss, the look on his face when we made love, his eyes which told me he loved me. These were the memories that kept me from moving on. I reminisced over how we had successfully managed to partner with each other starting a small company.

The hardest part about leaving the relationship was saying good bye to the lifestyle that I had grown accustomed too. The income that exceeded both our imaginations, the finer things of life that he provided me: and the new homes we built. We even had our own community of rental properties, numerous new cars and the luxury of many splendid vacations. But the thing that I desired most was his heart. The one thing he could not give. I convinced myself none of these things mattered if I was not happy.

I was adamant about leaving him, and this time, I refused to listen to anything he had to say. I refused to accept any more apologies. No amount of tears could change my mind. I was out of there!

I could sense this man praying. I saw something in his eyes. He seemed very sorrowful for what he had done, but my heart was like Pharaoh, hardened and all I wanted was out of the relationship. I refused to listen to anymore lies. Eighteen years had gone by and I was stuck in a relationship whose foundation was built on deceit and betrayal. I found myself not wanting to cry out to God. He looked as though he had taken a vacation on me. I could not feel His presence nor hear His voice. I nearly forgot that I was professing to be a Saint. In my sorrows and with my eyes centered on my problems, I found myself quickly moving to an "ain't." Realizing I was falling from the grace of God. I cried out to God to please help me, to save me, deliver me from the foes of the enemy, and not to allow the enemy to devour me.

In praying I told God that I would not leave the relationship mad, but would leave on a happy note.

As always, Dona' Trust and I decided to spend time together. This time we would spend this time in church. It did not matter that we were going to church. I did not trust him no further than I could see. Dona' had lied so much until, I believed he himself did not know truth if it was staring him in his face. He lied about everything, from the cars we rented, to the houses he sold, the life he lived, our marriage, the outside children he fathered, his age; everything was a lie.

The minister appeared to be preaching to us and about us. It was as though she had been at our home and had witnessed everything that had taken place between us. As she preached, my daughter pranced about trying to get my attention, but I refused to look her way.

When the sermon was completed, the Pastor called a prayer line and I made a wild dash to the altar. I needed the prayers of the saints to help carry me through the turmoil I was living. As I approached the altar, I noticed the reflection of a short, stocky, muscle bound man standing slightly behind me. It was Dona. To my surprise, he had made his way to the altar for prayer, something he had never done before.

As we stood patiently in the prayer line, God began ministering to the both us in such a way that it really got our attention. The minister instructed us to join hands and then she prophesied to us. She informed us that a Spirit of Division had been sent against our marriage in an attempt to cause me to fall out of the will of God. With this spirit, came a seducing spirit which was trying to pull Dona' from the marriage. This spirit was using my husband and did not want us to remain together.

The minister said, "I had become impatience and did not want to wait on God and any longer." She was indeed correct, because not only did I not want to wait on God, I was bent on helping Him out. God was moving too slow so I decided to speed up the process. As a matter of fact, God was moving so slow until I thought maybe He had caught a ride on a turtle's back. I had become bitter over Dona's admission to infidelity and had purposed in my heart to divorce him. But God saw the heart of Dona.

God instructed me to "stand still and to wait on Him for he was going to fix things between us." God said that He was in control and would not allow the enemy to destroy what He had joined together; "for what He had joined together let no man put asunder."

For a moment, I was okay in hearing from God and vowed to obey His voice. But the Adversary, Satan began whispering sweet nothing in my ears. As he talked to me, I found myself becoming angry with God. I threw question after question at Him.

My first question as usual was, "Why me Lord? Why must I stay with this man? Why must I be like Hosea, married to a man that has a whoredom spirit? Why must I stay with him when you have placed a clause in the Bible: just for me? Why must I preach the gospel? Why must I leave my job and career? Why have You chosen me to bear this burden?" Why must I stand and wait on You Lord, Lord why me?"

I prayed and I prayed. I prayed day in and day out. I begged God for mercy. I begged Him to please help me. I begged him to kill me: at least this would alleviate the pain I was in. I knew nothing else to do but pray, and at times this did not appear to be working.

My relationship with God told me prayer was the answer and faith unlocks the doors, but it appeared as though my prayers were unheard. I knew within my spirit man that God was able to do anything but fail and in His hand I yield every aspect of my life.

I prayed and I prayed. I prayed day in and day out. I begged God for mercy. I begged Him to help me in making the right decision as it pertained to my marriage.

In praying and waiting on the Lord for answers, I went to Him with a heart of repentance for questioning Him. In my heart I knew that He was my Father and because of this intimate relationship I was going to come out on top regardless of how it looked. My relationship with Him, lead me to believe that He would not allow the enemy to destroy me. He promised he would not put more on me than I could bear."

His word told me that He loved me enough to give His only begotten Son so that I could have a friend to take all my burdens too. I could count on His everlasting love because He is faithful.

For a while things appeared better between me and Dona' Trust. However, they were not. Dona' returned to his old tricks, after praying and seeking God for direction he said I could leave the relationship, but not without God warning Dona.' God instructed Dona to be trustful about his past however, he refused to yield to the voice of God, he continued to do his thing. It was as though he had no fear of God. I actually thought he had going mad.

God said I was free to go if I so desired. After trying for nearly a year to make things work between us, things got worse. I battled with my emotions in saying goodbye to a love that we had invested nearly twenty years in. I wanted to be free of all the confusion, deceit and lies, but how could I let go of the only love that I knew? A love that was crazy, deceitful: and a love that could betray me. I was tired, as a matter of fact; my tired was tired.

Kesia was having more difficulties with our breakup than I. It tore me to pieces watching her fret over what she was hearing about Dona' Trust in the streets. She wanted to know what was happening with her step-dad so she kept the phone line lit up. This was how she got the hook up or the "411," as she called it, through her cell phone which was her main source of communication.

Kesia must have felt sorry for me when she saw me struggling with so many issues and decided to move to Orlando to be closer to me. She was a blessing. It was as though God had sent her to be with me. When she first moved to Orlando, she had to stay with me but after about four months she found an apartment for her and her girls. After settling in her place, I had to move in with her. I had not only lost Dona, but the beautiful home that Dona and I purchased in which I lived had been foreclosed on. I was now homeless and had no place to go. I refused to go back to Dona. I was not about to be arrested for some foolish fight that might erupt between us.

Kesia's friends called her daily keeping her abreast of what Dona' Trust was doing. I asked her repeatedly not to tell me what she knew about him, but somehow she could not keep what she heard to herself. She would wrestle for days over gossip that she heard when all of a sudden she would burst in my room saying, "Mom I just got to tell you this." And from that point on she would let everything she heard rip.

When she finally accepted the fact that I had made up my mind not to return to the relationship, she was heart sick. She cried more that I did. She rehearsed Dona and I relationship over and over again trying to figure out what caused him to stray.

Her comment to me was "Mama, Dona Trust has been the only daddy that I have known. He has been in my life since I was fifteen and I can not believe this is happening to you again, she cried.' He bought me my first new car when I sixteen and gave Skeeter his first car too." I tried comforting her by telling her he was another child's father and not her biological daddy and this alone made a different in the choices he was making."

A year later, I packed my few belongings and left our home. A home that he purchased for me on my thirty fifth birthday. This home was bought immediately after I found out about the first child.

Dona' Trust hurriedly invited Imma Home Wrecker and her children to our home. As a matter of fact, I was not gone two days before he bought her to our home and rushed them off to meet his family. It was as though I had never been married to him at all. On Thanksgiving Day he took his new family on vacation to visit his out of town relatives. His family was very close and none of them seem to care how this would affect me, only a sister that lived hundreds of miles away. She called me daily trying to comfort me. She totally disagreed with her family in how they were handling the situation between me and Dona.

After all the wrong he had done to me, somewhere in the back of Dona's mind he thought I would continue in my role as his wife, even while he flaunted his mistress about the town in which we both lived, which was an even bigger insult. He made every attempt to reconcile with me. However, I was too angry with him to hear what he had to say. Each time he tried reconciling I would call his girlfriend letting her know. I was determine to show Dona' that I was not like the average woman and especially not like his girlfriend. I had made up my mind if I could not be his wife, I was not going to be his girlfriend and I surely was not about to sleep with him now that we were separated. It was as if, he really believed that I was going to tolerate his belligerent behavior.

Although we were separated for over a year, he kept pursuing me. If he found out I was in town he would come wherever I was.

Several times he visited me in Imma' vehicle just as he had done me, driving my truck to visit her. Our friends thought he had lost his mind when he showed up at their house in Imma's truck. I had gotten accustomed to his behavior and thought to myself, "what goes around will come around."

If I spent the weekend with my friends, Dona would be spotted riding up and down their street, especially if he recognized my truck. He would find a reason to stop by their house even if it was to give me the mail or to ask a question. Dona' never stopped calling, he was determined to show me that it wasn't over until he said so.

After getting over the initial shock of the affair, I responded to his calls because I did not want to harbor bitterness or hatred of heart, plus I was making every effort to move on with my life and still be friends with him.

At first this was very hard for me. If he called I would be very short in answering him, not saying very much. I remember our second New Years apart. This was the hardest New Years of them all. I was in Niagara Falls, New York when he called at twelve o'clock in the morning to be the first to wish me a "Happy New Year." When I realized that it was him all I could say was "thank you" and I hung up not allowing him to say anything else.

This went on for about nine months. My mother loved him and asked me to "please be nice to him." She sighed, "Don't be nasty when he calls, just listen to him and talk nice." I obeyed her and we slowly became friends again.

I was having a hard time with the hold situation. How could he want to talk to me when he had treated me so badly? Why would he continue calling me when he had what he wanted? His girlfriend children were calling him daddy and yet he expected me to smile through this mess.

Imma Home wrecker did not believe that he was still calling me. She thought it was I bothering Dona. If I returned his calls she would take the phone from him and argue at me. I told her that she needed to put her man on a dog chain. Dona' made most of his calls from his vehicle, but by the time I returned his calls; she would answer the phone loosing it. Once she heard my voice she called me an "old ass." I was not insulted by this comment in the least little bit, as a matter of fact it was funny. I did not respond to her comment but thought to myself at least I had lived to become what she considered "an old ass." I had lived through many disappointments and had successfully overcome all of them, and had come out looking excellent and smelling like a rose for "an old ass." I said to myself "you better pray that you live to become an "Old ass," because at the rate you are going some man's wife is going to hang your young immature behind from a tree."

Breaking up homes was her expertise. I later learned that mines was not her first.

Imma Home Wrecker was living in a fantasy world. She felt she had taken Dona from me but she had not, she had received something that I freely gave her. Imma was certain that she had Dona' wrapped around her little finger and that she would be able to tame him. In her narrow mind she believed I had not done my job as his wife and that he loved her and only her because she had mothered his child.

She refused to see Dona as he actually was. He loved women, and there would always be a woman standing in between them. If it was not his mother, (the diva) it would be Tammy, if not Tammy, Kim; he would always have an extra woman as his ace of diamond. She was not the first to mother his children and probably would not be the last. I was blessed not to have been caught in that trap. I could walk away never looking back at him, but she like the others were not that fortunate.

Dona' was not a man that wanted to be tamed. He was a man about control, especially the females he dated. He allowed a woman to think that she was in control. He would even allow her to boss him around until he was fed up. He would permit her to rant and raid not saying a word, all the while planning his next game plan. When he was caught being mischievous he could put on an act, letting his emotions flow like a river of water. He could cry at the drop of a hat, looking ever so sad and walking away looking as though he had lost his best friend: leading a sister to believe that she had conquered his heart. However, just as she thought she had won his heart, he would drop a bomb on her. Every woman he was involved with soon found herself awakening to this rude awaiting when he walked away from her.

I too was nearly caught in that trap. It would be nearly twenty years before I would take inventory of his past. It would cost me a shattered heart. A heart so broken and shattered until I thought it would never heal. My heart was like a cup when it had been dropped numerous times. After being dropped so many times; the cracks could not be put back together again.

I cried day in and day out, everything made me cry. I had never cried from anything before this. Before meeting Dona I thought my heart had turned to stone. And I truly thought my tear ducts has dried up. I did not think they had any water in them. However, after Dona got through with me every buried memory came to surface. I had never cried from the break up of my first marriage, nor had I shed a tear over the second, but I cried a river of tears over all three men of my past. I had never cried tears for Beat Em Up nor Cheater John, now some twenty years later, I was crying uncontrollably. I was crying about all the hurt I had reccived during life. I cried something awful about my parents not wanting me, the many bad things that my mother said to me when she was angry. Tears streamed down my face as I thought about the men that had mistakenly taken my love for granted. Tears came from everywhere. I cried so much until I had formed a lake called "Lake Joanna," so many tears were locked inside of me. It was as though someone had unlatched a fountain within me.

I cried in church, in the store, to my friends, to my children, to my pastor and even while walking in the park. I had never cried so much in all of my life. My world had come to an end, so I felt. I was forced to leave the marriage, never returning to Dona's vicious unstable world.

A year after moving to Orlando, Kesia expired. Satan submitted a Spirit of death upon her, my oldest daughter. I knew she had health problems which would eventually take her life, but I was not prepared when death suddenly crept up on her a day before my fiftieth birthday. She had become my best friend and confidant, someone that I talked to about everything. She was the fire at the end of the candle that burnt between me and Dona.

When she expired, I wasn't sure if my mind was stable enough to handle her death. I had lost the two most important people of my life, my husband whom I freely handed over to another woman; and Kesia, my oldest child, who was my best friend.

I cried out in agony, Lord! Why Me? I prayed and prayed. The more I prayed the worst things appeared. My spirit man could not take any more and felt as though it was broken.

It was in my brokenness that I came to know that God is a great and merciful God. In my brokenness, I came to understand that God was right there for me and, had outlined my life according to His plans. In doing so, I may have had to endure emotional hardships, pain, suffering and disappointments, but with each of them I overcame. I learned to trust God and I became free of those things that had me bound. In the midst of confusion, I found clarity and now I am able to live a life that is more in balance. I shall continue to live according to God's commandments and I shall "Stand still and see His Salvation."

I believed that *"The Lord was perfecting those things concerneth me* as according to Psalms 138:8, NIV. And because of this, I now have a peace that passes all understanding. Yes, in life I must cry sometime, it is written:" ***Weeping may endure for a night, but joy comes in the morning."***

Serving God has not been easy, but has been challenging. At times, I did not think I would make it. I have had moments when my trials were so severe I could not pray. I could only moan and groan as I lifted my head up towards heaven with tears in my eyes.

As I prayed Satan would sometimes send his little demonic spirits upon me. But I kept on praying. I purposed in my heart to hold on to God's unchanging hand.

The one thing that carried me and caused me not to succumb to Satan's will, was grasping that God is faithful and is very real and knowing that His nature is not about wickedness.

In moments of despair, it was in His Word that I found solitude and truth. Over time, I have learned not to put confident in man, for man will deceive you. The Bible says,

***"It is better to trust in the Lord than
to put confidence in man"*** *(Psalm
118:8, NIV).*

In serving God and through all of the many difficult situations, I found God to be truthful and trustworthy. For He said, ***"He would never leave me nor forsake me"*** *(Hebrews 13:5, NIV).*

He's been true to His Word: for he has not forsaken me nor have he left me. He has promised to be with me ***"Even unto the end of the world"*** *(Matthew 28:20, NIV)* and he has done just that.

In being faithful and true to His every word, He is not like man. He will never break your heart, deceive you, lie to you, or cheat on you for Satan.

For the first time in my life, I am free. It took me a while to see the blessings of God in all of this, but gradually God began to reveal himself. I have no man in my life that refuses to commit. Nor do I have one that brings his issues to me, no job to stress me and especially no debt. I am free, praise the Lord I'm free! The chains of bondage have been broken from my life and I have a new look on life, new walk and a new talk. I could not see what God was allowing the enemy to do for me, but now I see what God was doing. I found peace, peace that passes all understanding. God took those tears of mine and bottled them up. He took those ashes of mines and turned them into beauty. I serve an awesome God, who is worthy to be praised.

Psalms 56:9 declares, ***"When I cry unto thee, then shall mine enemies turn back: this I know; for God is for me (NIV).***

10

WEEPING MAY ENDURE FOR A NIGHT

Beneath the shadow of life lies a stream of peace, happiness, and joy: but, crossing the river of change sometimes awaits hurt and pain.

David wrote in Psalm 34:19, *"Many are the affliction of the righteous: but the Lord delivereth him out of them all" (NIV).*

From reading the scripture, David was experiencing numerous problems. Although his troubles were many, he kept his faith in knowing that no matter what he was going through, God was God, and in His own timing He would rescue him from his afflictions.

Like David, we are not exempt from suffering, and there will be many days in which we will be inflicted with some sort of pain. Sometimes, the pain so severe until we will weep, and at times the pain maybe so deep: causing us to only groan. Regardless of the situation God is able to fix things and deliver us from our afflictions. Psalm 30:5 declares, *"weeping may endure for a night, but joy cometh in the morning."*

Weeping is a process in which each of us will do, it is an essential part of life. Very seldom do we cry tears of joy, but oftentimes we weep because we have been wounded.

Being wounded is a time of discomfort. A time of anguish,

heartbreak, hurt and a time in which we feel burdensome. It is a time when we cry and make decisions concerning issues of life.

Crying can be viewed as a time of grief or a time when we allow ourselves to heal from dis-stressful situations.

When we encounter circumstances beyond our ability to handle, it is during this time we should turn to God. Maybe God is trying to get our attention, or He could be trying our patience. Most people would say that Satan is trying to destroy them. We know that he comes to "steal, kill and to destroy." Steal our joy, kill our happiness, and destroy our chance of having eternal life.

It is at this point, where many believers fail the test and give up in despair. They become overwhelmed, confused, angry, bitter, and lose focus. Many times Christians turn to their own understanding just as I did when circumstances of life over took me. They forget to wait on God. They forget the word which states, **"God does not always strive with man"** *(Gen 6:3, NIV).*

They do not remember that it was God, the creator of the heavens and earth that created man after his own likeness and in His image and it was He who has given Satan permission to test and try our faith. Since He is the creator of all things, He does know what we have need of. Many people do not remember that Satan cannot do anything without permission from God. Christians should therefore focus on the Word of God and not their problems. However, this is easier said than done.

Problems are like change, they come to either make us better or they make us worse. They come to build us up or to tear us down. Whatever the reason, as Christians and as people in general, we must trust God without a shadow of a doubt. We must walk after righteousness regardless of our circumstances and situations.

When Christians walk according to the Word of God, we know that whatever the situation and whatever Satan send down the path of life, God has our back. In other words, we are covered by the blood of Jesus from head to toe. Our belief in God tells us:

For we know that all things work together for good to them that love God, to them who are called according to his purpose (Psalms 8: 28 NIV, italics).

Therefore we are assured that *all* things are working together for our good despite what it looks like to the natural eye. In spite of what our emotions are telling us: Despite what Satan is whispering in our ears and no matter what we may have to endure we must positively endorse our faith with the Word of God.

With every trail and each tribulation, God is leading us towards His perfect will. Our suffering is only for a moment, and is done to make us stronger or to move us into spiritual growth and maturity.

Jeremiah 1:5, said: *"Before I formed thee in the belly I knew thee."* Therefore before the foundation of the world was established, it can be said that God preordained the events of our life.

Weeping therefore is a process and is something that everyone will do in order to heal. We weep for many reasons, the lost of a job, the death of a loved one, a sick child, separation, divorce and sin.

Most people do not realize that many of their problems are the result of sin and could have been avoided. Sin has been known to have its place in making a person weep. There were numerous people throughout the Bible that wept. They like us, cried over relationship, the lost of a child, a brother, and other matters dear to their heart.

David wept over the death of his illegitimated child when it died because of his sins. Therefore when sin is committed there will be grief; and from our grief there will be suffering.

David sinned against God and Uriah by lying with his wife, Bathsheba. Shortly afterwards, she learned that she was pregnant with his child.

When Bathsheba informed David that she was with child, his immediate response was to cover up his sin with a lie. He summoned Uriah the Hittite and demanded him to *"go to his house and wash his feet" (II Samuel 11:8, NIV).* Uriah did not do as David commanded; however, what he did was, *"slept at the door of the king's house with all the servants."* When David received news that Uriah did not go home as instructed, David questioned him as to why he did not follow his instructions (8, 9, 10, NIV).

II Samuel 11:11 declares that Uriah responded by saying:
The ark, and Israel, and Judah, abide in tents; and my lord Joab, and the servants of my lord, are encamped in the open fields; shall I then go into mine house, to eat and to drink, and to lie with my wife? as thou livest, and as thy soul liveth, will not do this thing (NIV italic added).

David realized that his plan had not worked and he nevertheless instructed Uriah to stay another day in Jerusalem. During this stay, David summoned him to his palace, feeding him, getting him drunk *"and at even he went out to lie on his bed with the servants of his lord, but did not go down to his house" (13, NIV).*

David did not want anyone to know of his wrong doing, he went as far as planning the death of Uriah. *"He wrote a letter to Joab, saying: Set ye Uriah in the forefront of the hottest battle, and retire ye from him, that he may be smitten, and die" (14, 15, NIV).*

Joab did as he was mandated and when Uriah died, he sent a messenger to David telling him Uriah the Hittite was dead. Soon thereafter, Bathsheba received word that her husband Uriah was dead, she mourned for him (26, NIV).

"And when the mourning period was past, David sent and fetched her to his house, and she became his wife, and bare him a son. But the thing that David had done displeased the Lord" (27, NIV).

The Lord was so displeased with him until he sent a prophet by the name of Nathan to his home. During this visit, he spoke to David in parables concerning the sin he had committed.

At first, David did not recognize that the story was about himself, but after a moment Nathan informed him that *"thou art the man" (7, NIV).*

He continued his prophesy by saying,

> *Thus saith the Lord of Israel, I anointed thee king over Israel, and I delivered thee out of the hand of Saul; I gave thee thy master's house, and thy master's wives into thy bosom, and gave thee the house of Israel and of Judah; and if that had been too little, I would have given unto thee such and such things. Wherefore hast thou despised the commandment of the Lord, to do evil in his sight? thou hast killed Uriah the Hittite with the sword, and hast taken his wife to be thy wife, and hast slain him with the sword of the children of Ammon (8, 9, NIV, italic added).*

As a punishment to David for the sin committed against Uriah, *God said that the sword would never depart from David's house; "Because thou hast despised me, and hast taken the wife of Uriah the Hittite to be thy wife."*

God punished him by causing evil to come against his house

and by taking away his wives and giving them to his neighbor. God said unto David because **"Thou gave occasion to the enemies of the Lord to blaspheme, the child that is born unto thee shall surely die"** *(II Samuel 12:11, 14, NIV).*

When Nathan had done all that the Lord commanded him, he left the house of David. "And the Lord struck the child that Uriah's wife bare unto David and it was very sick" (15, NIV).

David went to the Lord in prayer concerning this child. "He fasted, went in, laid all night upon the earth" (16, NIV).

The Bible says that "The elders of his house arose, went to him, picking him off the ground. He refused to get up, nor did he eat" (17, NIV).

On the seventh day, the child died. David noticed his servants whispering, he knew in his heart that the child had expired. He got up from the ground, washed himself, anointed his body, changed clothes and went into the house of the Lord and worshipped Him.

David's weeping was a result of his sin. It was sin that could have been avoided if he had not been persuaded by his fleshly desires. His sin caused years of grief and suffering for his entire family. Generations later, one can see consequences for David's behavior. Scriptures give us the understanding that as a result of sin David's family was inflicted with generational curses.

11

THE DEATH OF LAZARUS

Mary wept for her brother, Lazarus when he died. In her heart she believed that if Jesus had been there while Lazarus was sick, he would not have died.

When Jesus saw that she and the Jewish people were crying "he groaned in the spirit, and was troubled." He asked the question, "Where have ye laid him?" Mary slowly walked toward the grave of Lazarus, with her head bowed and tears streaming down her face, and her hands folded across her chest, looking helpless at Lazarus's grave.

From a distance she could hear the crowd as they eagerly followed after them. Many of them were crying as well. Jesus said unto her in a soft whisper, "Show me where he lay." And when he saw Lazarus's grave, He wept too.

The people cried for Lazarus when he died, and they watched with disbelief as **Jesus shouted,** Lazarus! Lazarus, Come forth from thy sleep! Death take your hands off of him!" said Jesus. All of a sudden, the earth began to give way, rocking and moving as though there was a sudden earthquake. Out came Lazarus's hands, next they saw his feet pushing and shoveling the earth from around him.

Lazarus got up from his grave, the clothing in which he wore unraveled.

The crowd hurriedly gathered around the grave of Lazarus. To their surprise, they witnessed Lazarus getting up from his grave.

The people voices roared out as he came forth. A number of them hissed and others sighed as they watched in disbelief as Lazarus got up from his grave.

Among them were those individuals who believed in the works of Jesus, tears of joy streamed down their faces as they rejoiced and gave praise to Almighty God for his mighty works. Also in the crowd were those individuals who did not believe in Jesus, they were spectators and it was for their benefit that Jesus raised Lazarus from the grave. He performed this miraculous event to demonstrate to those that did not believe that God was a deliverer even unto death.

Mary rejoiced over the awakening of her brother, and in seeing him she counted it to her joy. She knew that with God nothing was impossible.

Weeping is a form of releasing or expressing pain and sorrow by means of crying. Jesus was not exempted from weeping and therefore as men and women, boys or girls we will have our day for weeping and crying.

Joy came to both David and Bethsheba and Mary, Lazarus's sister: not at that moment, but at a later time, nevertheless it came. David no doubt rejoiced when Bathsheba became pregnant with their second child. This child would be selected by God to build His temple.

The people no doubt cried for Lazarus when he died, marveled when Jesus raised him from the dead and rejoiced when he got up from his grave. Behind every tear there is joy. Joy does come in the morning light.

12

COUNT IT ALL JOY

Have you ever laid in bed thinking about the hand life had dealt you? The many changes you had experienced, the people you have met, and the places you've gone?

How many times have you mourned because you believed life had been unfair? The children may have gone astray, the husband may have left you for another, your funds may have been depleted, your health maybe failing or you may have just lost your job. However; Rev 21:4 declares:

And God shall wipe away all tears from their eyes; and there shall be no more death, neither sorrow, nor crying, neither shall there be anymore pain...(NIV, italic added).

In other words, God has promised to put an end to crying, death, sorrow and pain. One day, these things shall be no more.

Have you ever stopped to rejoice over how good God has been to you despite what you may have going through even when the enemy had you over a barrel, nevertheless He blessed you?

As I sit reminiscing over my life, I can say that I've been blessed even when there were adversities in my life. There were days when I thought I just could not make it. There were nights when all I could do was trust God and Praise Him for his goodness.

Looking back over my life, I can see God's hand as He steered me in the directions of His plans. Although there were tedious moments, God never left me entirely to the enemy. When I fell short due to my flesh, he did not leave me. When He should have left me, He did not. When I was visited by death, He made death behave. When I was hungry, He fed me. When I was thirsty, He gave me water from a living spring.

When I was heavy burdened, He said unto me *"come unto me all that are heavy burden and I shall give you rest."* When I felt all alone, He was there. When I was weak, He strengthened me. When I was sad, He gave me joy.

When I was in despair, He gave me hope. When I was in bondage, He set me free. When I was sick in mind, he healed me. When I could not see Him, His *"word became a lamp unto my feet and a light unto my path." (Psalms 119:105, NIV).*

When I was confused, He gave me truth. When my enemies thought they had devoid me, He made them my footstool. When I was naked, He clothed me. And when I was wrapped in sin, He pardoned me.

I began to count it all joy when I realized that I could have been dead and sleeping in my grave. I gave thanks to God for how He watched over me and allowed me to safely return home, especially during those nights when I had been too high (on drugs) to realize where I was.

I counted it all joy for those men whom I was in relationship with and for the way they misused me, abused me and most of all for their lustfulness of spirit. For their inability to commit: roaming eyes, abusive nature and their unfaithfulness. It was these things that helped me to seek after a God who is faithful in all of His doing.

It was their immoral behavior that taught me the importance of morals and that it was necessary that God be a significant part of my life. The Bible is real in all aspects. For it reads, *"It is better to put thou confidence in the Lord than to trust in man, for man will deceive you" (Psalms 118:8, NIV).*

Lord, Why Me?

I count it all joy for the lessons in deceit, for it taught me the importance of not deceiving anyone. The hurt, pain, suffering and disappointment it creates should be avoided at all cost.

I counted it joy for the biological father who was not there for me as a child, because God, the Father and creator of all things taught me how to lean and to depend on Him.

I counted it joy when I was employed and God instructed me to "leave the job," but I refused to obey Him and did my own thing, learning afterwards when God gives a command, we are to obey. From that experience, I've learned that *"the just shall live by faith and not by sight"* (Habakkuk 2: 4, NIV). God has supplied all of my needs just as He said he would.

I counted it all joy when I witnessed God providing all of my needs according to His own timing. I count it all joy when I had no money, bills were in need of being paid yet, God taught me that He would take care of me. It was during these times that God reinforced His word, when He said:

"His thoughts are not our thoughts,
neither are our ways his ways"
(Isaiah 55:8, NIV).

I had faith enough to believe that God would bring me through, but I thought it should have been done my way and not according to His way nor his timing.

I counted it all joy for the six beautiful children God gave to me, to nurture, to care for and to lead them to His throne so that they can become servant of the cross.

I counted it all joy for two of my children who were sentenced to prison for an extended period of time. Prison is a place of confinement, however, if Joseph and Paul, Biblical prisoners found their purpose and destiny; so shall those children that God loaned to me, they shall do the same.

I counted it all joy for the sexual abuse I was subjected to as a child. I am sure it kept me from becoming a "Lady of the Night."

I count it all the joy for the last rape for it was during that rape, I heard the voice of God speaking to my spirit man. Leaving me to comprehend that God is real.

I counted it all joy for the number of years I was a welfare recipient, now I can tell those mothers who feel trapped by "the system" how to overcome and obtain an education.

I counted it all joy for the physical abuse I received as a wife, because I can relate to young women all over the world about what signs to look for in an abusive relationship. I can suggest and encourage them to "get out," do not take the abuse from the abuser, he/she is trying to control you.

I counted it all joy for my Children's father, who gave his life to Christ after we met, when no one thought he would change. For it was during those early morning hours" that the Word of God penetrated his heart, as I read the Bible to him while he was "high on drugs."

I count it all joy for the third relationship, his immoral and negative behavior caused me to pray, trust God, come to God with my whole heart and allow God to order my steps.

I count it all joy for the interlopers that stepped in, ruined my home, for they made me look at life from a different perspective. I learned that if God had joined someone together they would not be put asunder, therefore; if a marriage fails, it evidently was not in the will of God.

I counted it all joy for the disappointments, hurt, pain and suffering I received by the hands of those that were supposed to love me, but did not. For it was these people that taught me how to love: to show forgiveness to those that trespassed against me.

I count it all joy when I spent time locked up in a mental hospital, for it was there that I began to recognize that God is **Jehovah Rapha,** *"The Lord that heals"(Exo 15:26).*

I counted it all joy for the peace of mind that God has given me in knowing that He is my all in all, my everything, my comforter. ***He is Jehovah Shalom, the Lord our Peace** (Judges 6:24, NIV).*

I counted it all joy for when I was a lost sheep to a world of sin, ***He was and still is Jehovah-Raah, "The Lord my Shepherd,"** (Psalms 23:1, NIV).*

I counted it all joy because when I was in need, ***He supplied all of my needs according to his riches in glory, He is Jehovah Jireh, my provider** (Gen 22:14, NIV).*

I counted it all joy for how He sent his only Son into this world to redeem that which Satan thought he had taken from Adam. ***He is Jehovah-Elohim, the Lord God, the Redeemer and creator** (Genesis 2:4, NIV).*

I counted it all joy for when He picked me up from a world of sin, placed my feet on solid ground, He sanctified me ***and became Jehovah Mekaddeskum, The Lord who sanctifies** (Exodus 31:13, NIV).*

I counted it all joy for when I was all alone and had no where to turn ***God is Jehovah-Shammah, The Lord who is there, and everpresence** (Ezekiel 48: 35, NIV).*

I counted it all joy when the enemy told me "God is not real." I looked around and saw His marvelous works in the sun, moon, stars, and the sky above as they shined so very bright. He is the light of the world and can be seen even in our darkest moments.

I counted it all joy for everything that life has dealt me. I counted it all joy for my Lord and Savior, Jesus Christ who is ***Jehovah-Jeshoshua Christos the anointed one** (Ephesians 1:20-21 NIV).* The one who died on Calvary: so that I could become sanctified, following in his footsteps.

I counted it all joy for the enemy who thought he had killed me; God stepped in and said "no you will not, her work has not been completed". I count it all joy for every trial and tribulation sent my way. For God is a deliverer me.

For it is written in the Book of Isaiah 43:2 ***"When thou (I)*** *passest through the waters, I (God) will be with thee (me); and through the rivers, they shall not overflow me: when thou (I) walkest through the fire, thou (I) shall not burned; neither shall the flame kindle upon thee (me)" (NIV).*

13

GOD IS A DELIVERER

As I set sail upon the sea of life, it appears as though my ship is without a captain. The tides are high: the sea was rough and with every step was like sinking sand. Placing my feet into the depths of the water, I found myself sinking fast. And like Peter, I too cried out "Lord, save me" *(Matthew 14:15, NIV)*.

Riding on a mustard seed of faith, and calling upon a God whom I know to be a deliverer, I watched as the mountains slowly fade behind the eclipse of my faith. This mountain appears to be sinking sand, but I, like Peter have built my house upon a solid rock.

I've learned that *"Many are the affliction of the righteous: but the Lord is able to deliver him out of all of them" (Psalms 34:19, NIV)*.

The Lord remembered David and all his afflictions, and *"Clothed his enemies with shame: but upon himself his crown flourish" (Psalms 132:1, 18, NIV)*.

On three different occasions Saul tried to capture David. The Bible says that David declared in Psalms 54:3,

> *For strangers are risen up against me, and oppressors seek after my soul: they have not set God before them (NIV, italics added)*.

Saul in all of his wickedness believed that God had delivered David into his hand. But David kept inquiring of the Lord concerning his safety and from his prayers God continued to direct him.

Saul attempted to seize David again in the wilderness of En-gedi. The Bible declares that:

> **Saul took three thousand chosen**
> **men out of Israel, and went to seek**
> **David and his men upon the rocks of**
> **the wild goats** (I Sam 24:3 NIV, *italic added*).

David, a righteous man and one who could have destroyed Saul, refused to lay a finger upon the king, "the Lord's anointed" (I Samuel 24:10, NIV, italic added).

> **He declared in Psalms 57: 6, They**
> **have prepared a net for my steps,**
> **my soul is bowed down: they have**
> **digged a pit before me, into the midst**
> **whereof they are fallen themselves.**

Saul in his pursuit of David, felt the need to rest. As he lay sleeping in the wilderness, David and his men stumbled upon them:

> **David's men said unto him, Behold**
> **the day of which the Lord said unto**
> **thee, Behold, I will deliver thine**
> **enemy into thine that thou mayest**
> **do to him as it shall seem good unto**
> **thee. Then David arose, and cut off**
> **the skirt of Saul's robe privily.**
> (I Samuel 24:4, NIV, *italic added*).

Although, David knew that Saul desired to kill him, he purposed in his heart not to render evil for evil against the king. Psalms 7: 3-5 says, that David cried:

> **O Lord my God, if I have done this;**
> **if there be iniquity in my hands;**
> **If I have rewarded evil unto him that**

> *was at peace with me; (yea, I have*
> *delivered him that was without cause*
> *is mine enemy:)*
> **Let the enemy persecute my soul,**
> **and take it; yea, let him tread down**
> **my life upon the earth, and lay mine**
> **honour in the dust** *(italic added).*

David appeared to be praying a prayer of mercy. In his heart he had not intentionally set out to cause injury to anyone. He asked God to allow his enemy to do as they wish with his soul if he had done evil to anyone that was at peace with him.

Saul tried capturing David for the third time in the wilderness of Ziph, but was not successful. David devised a plan of escape. He sent spies out to determine Saul's whereabouts. Upon learning where Saul was and as "he and his men lay sleeping within the trench: and his spear stuck in the ground at his bolster" (I Samuel 26: 7, NIV), David could have killed the king, but refused to do so and spared his life again.

As David and Abishai searched the cave, he said to Abishai, **Destroy him not: for who can stretch forth his hand against the Lord's anointed and be guiltless?** *(vv 9: NIV, italics added).*

David furthermore said, As the Lord liveth, the Lord shall smite him; or his day shall come to die; or he shall descend in to battle, and perish. *(I Samuel 26:10, NIV, italic added).*

Instead of killing the king, David took Saul's "spear and the cruse of water" and left the place where the king and his men were a slept (I Samuel 26:12, NIV).

Although, David was stressed over Saul's desire to kill him, he refused to harm the king when the opportunity presented itself. Instead he continued to call upon the Lord. As he lay resting in the confidence of the Lord, he said in his heart:

> **I shall now perish one day by the**
> **hand of Saul: there is nothing**

better for me than that I should speedily escape into the land of the Philistines; and Saul shall despair of me, to seek me any more in any coast of Israel: so shall I escape out of his hand. (I Samuel 27:1, NIV, italic added).

David most likely asked the question; "Lord, Why Me? What have I done to be treated as such? I've done all that the king has asked of me." I have faithfully served him. I even killed Goliath the giant whom his men were afraid. I am married to one of his daughters, still he sought to destroy me. I have played the harp to ward off evil spirits from the King, and yet he hates me without a cause. Lord, why me?" "Lord, I have even had to play crazy just to avoid the wrath of Saul? Lord! Why Me?"

David knew in his heart that the Lord was able to deliver him out of the hands of his enemies. Throughout all of his despair, he continued to trust God. His relationship with God was of confidence that He was a deliverer. He said in Psalms 3:6, NIV, italic added:

I will not be afraid of ten thousand of people, that have set themselves against me round about. Arise, O Lord; save me, O my God: for thou hast smitten all mines enemies upon the cheek bone; thou hast broken the teeth of the ungodly.

The Bible makes it clear that God answered David's prayer. Like Job he was sure that God would rescue him in His own timing.

Saul died by his own hands and David became the next ruler of Israel, where he remained king, until his son Solomon began to reign.

God is a deliver and He has always been. The Bible proves indisputable facts as to the number of people He rescued from terrible conditions. He was a deliver for the people of the Bible as He is a deliver for people of our tine.

14

MOSES, CHOSEN DELIVERER OF THE ISRAELITES

Moses, the adopted son of Pharaoh's daughter, was chosen by God to deliver the Israelites from the slavery of Pharaoh.

For years, the Israelites cried out to God for their freedom, without avail. One day while Moses was monitoring the suffering of his people, he saw an Egyptian being physical abused. When no one was paying attention, Moses killed the Egyptian and buried him in the sand. On the next day as Moses observed the men at work, one of them asked: "Why did you kill that man?" When Pharaoh heard what was done, his desire was to kill Moses. Moses out of fear took flight to the land of Midian, where he resided for forty years.

As time passed, the children of Israel continued to cry out to God for their freedom. *"God heard their crying, and remember the promise that he made with Abraham, Isaac and Jacob"*(Exodus 2:23-24, NIV).

One day while Moses was taking care of the flock of Jethro, his father-in-law, an angel of the Lord appeared unto him in a flame out of the midst of a bush (Exodus 3:1, NIV, italic added).

And the Lord said, I have surely seen
the affliction of my people which are
in Egypt, and have heard their cry

> *by reason of their taskmasters; for I know their sorrows;*
> *And I am come down to deliver them out of the hand of the Egyptians, and to bring them out of that land unto a good land and a large, unto a land flowing with milk and honey...*
> (Exodus 3:7-8, NIV, italic added).
> ***Come now therefore, and I will send thee unto Pharaoh, that thou mayest bring forth my people the children of Israel out of Egypt*** *(vv 10, NIV, italic added).*

Moses felt ill-equipped in performing this assignment and began telling God about his inability to do the task. But God did not listen to his excuses nor did He change His mind. Instead He prepared a way in which Moses could effectively do the job.

Moses immediately began to prepare for his journey back to Egypt. He encouraged his wife to gather a few of their belongings, called Aaron, his brother and off they went to rescue the children of Israel.

Upon returning to Egypt to meet with Pharaoh, the Egyptian king, God forewarned him of the challenges he would face.

> ***And the Lord said unto Moses, When thou goest to return into Egypt, see that thou do all those wonders before Pharaoh, which I have put in thine hand: but I will harden his heart, that he shall not let the people go***
> *(Exodus 4: 21, NIV, italics added).*

When Moses approached Pharaoh, his heart was hardened just as God said it would be. ***And Pharaoh said unto Moses, "Who do you think this God is that I should do as he has said, I know***

***not the God of Israel? And I will not let Israel go** (Exodus 5:2, NIV, italic added).*

Pharaoh's heart became hardened even towards the people of the land, in his anger he commanded them to work with their bare hands and no equipment.

> ***Then the officers of the children of Israel came and cried unto Pharaoh, saying, Wherefore dealest thou thus with thy servants?** (vv 15, NIV).*
> ***There is no straw given unto thy servants, and they say to us make brick: and behold, thy servants are beaten; but the fault is in thine own people** (vv 16, NIV).*

When Moses heard what Pharaoh had done to the children of Israel, he went before the Lord and asked, "Lord why hast thou allowed evil to come upon these people. Why have thou sent me"? "Lord, why me?

And the Lord spake unto Moses saying: ***"you should now witness what I shall do to Pharaoh: Go back to him and tell him that I said to let the children of Israel go"*** *(Exodus 6:11, NIV).*

Prior to Moses doing as God commanded him, he felt the need to remind the Lord of his weaknesses. And Moses said unto the Lord:

> ***I am of uncircumcised lips, and how shall Pharaoh hearken unto me?** (vv 30, NIV, italics added).*

Moses evidently forgot that God, the great "I AM" was in control of everything. In his moment of anxiety, he failed to realize that God not only created the heavens and the earth, but made Pharaoh too" (Genesis 1:26, NIV).

To ease Moses mind and to erase his fears, God said unto him, ***"Moses I need you to do as I have commanded you to do, for I*** *shall send your brother Aaron with you and he shall be my voice piece to Pharaoh" (Exodus 7:1, NIV).*

God said unto Moses, there is one thing that you need to keep in mind, *"I will harden Pharaoh's heart, and multiply my signs and wonders in the land of Egypt" (vv 3, NIV).*

Prepare yourself because *"Pharaoh will not listen to you for there are some things in which I the Lord God must do so that the Egyptians shall know that I am the Lord, "who shall bring the children of Israel out of the land of Egypt" (vv 4, 5, NIV).*

God, in being an all knowing God, took the liberty of warning both Moses and Aaron that Pharaoh would ask that a miracle be performed. Pharaoh in his disbelief of God no doubt thought that Moses would try to trick them but, instead God instructed Aaron to take his rod and to throw it down and when he does it came a serpent (vv 9, NIV).

Moses and Aaron did as the Lord God commanded but Pharaoh was not impressed in the least little bit. *He immediately summoned 'the wise men and the sorcerers, who were the magicians of Egypt" (vv 11, NIV).*

When these wise men saw what was done, they throw down their rods and watched in disbelief and fear as "Aaron's rod swallowed up their rods" (vv 12, NIV).

> *And he hardened Pharaoh's heart,*
> *that he hearkened not unto them; as*
> *the Lord had said.*
> *And the Lord said unto Moses,*
> *Pharaoh's heart is hardened, he*
> *refuseth to let the people go. (vv 13,*
> *14, NIV, italics added).*

Throughout Moses trial, God continued to harden Pharaoh's heart. Yet, God required Moses to approach him. When the Israelites were finally freed, Moses still had to contend with opposition on every end.

God had given him people that were complainers, grumblers and murmurs who were vocal throughout the journey. As a matter of fact, Moses became so frustrated with them until he lost his cool, and out of anger disobeyed a command from God.

I am sure that Moses must have said unto God, "Lord, Why Me"? Why have I been given the job of going before Pharaoh the king?

> For *"I am not eloquent, neither heretofore, nor since thou hast spoken unto thy servant: but I am slow of speech, and of a slow tongue"* (Exodus 4:10, NIV italics added).

I can heard the Lord as he answered Moses when he said unto him:

> ***Who hath made man's mouth? or who has maketh the dumb, or deaf, or seeing, or the blind? have not I the Lord?*** (Exodus 4:11, NIV, italics added).

Now get up and be about My business. Stop giving me excuses **"for I will be with thy mouth, and teach thee what thou shall say"** (vv 12, NIV).

Moses no doubt went to the Lord asking, Lord! Why Me? **"The children of Israel have not hearkened (listened) to me; how then shall Pharaoh hear me, who am of uncircumcised lips? Lord, who am I to go to the king?** (vv 12 : NIV).

The Bible declares in verse 13 that the **"Lord said unto Moses and Aaron, and gave them charge unto the children of Israel, and unto Pharaoh king of Egypt, to bring the children out of the land of Egypt"** (vv 13: NIV).

I can imagine Moses saying unto the Lord God, as he came to the place at the Red Sea, Lord! Why me? What must I do now?

We are surrounded by water on every side. When I turn to the east, there's water, when I look to the west, there is water, when I face the south, there is water and Lord when I move to the north I can see nothing but a body of water surrounding the people that you have given me to lead. "Lord! Why Me?"

As Moses talked with God, I can hear him say, "Pharaoh's army is quickly approaching and we have no where to turn. The people are shivering with fear as the sound of horses and voices of soldiers rumble from behind. He cried out, Lord! what must I do?"

Jehovah God, said in a loud, voice *"Moses why are you crying out to me'? You should be speaking to the children of Israel that they go forward. Moses! Lift up thy rod and stretch out thine hand over the sea, and divide it: and the children of Israel shall go on dry ground through the midst of the sea"* (vv 15, 16 NIV).

Moses did all that the Lord commanded him but not without challenges. On numerous occasions he questioned God because the assignment seemed complicated. And throughout his journey to the promise land, as leader and shepherd of the sheep, I believe he asked God, Lord Why Me?

Although, Moses may have thought that the task was tedious, he nevertheless obeyed God, went back to Pharaoh, and witnessed God do as he promised Abraham, Isaac, and Jacob. He delivered them out of the land of Egypt.

15

BARAK AND DEBORAH

Deborah was appointed by God to deliver and lead the people of Israel as they fought against Sisera.

She was a prophetess, the wife of Lapidoth and the first female who had been spiritually appointed to judge and rule Israel.

Judges 5:7 declares she was "a mother of Israel,"who sent for and called for Barak of Naphtali (NIV).

Deborah prophesied to Barak instructing him to: *"Go towards Mount Tabor and take with thee ten thousands men....and God will draw unto thee to the river Kishon Sisera, the captain of Jabin's army, with chariots and his multitude; and I will deliver him unto thine hand" (4:6-7, NIV).*

Barak agreed with Deborah but not without hesitation. *"He said unto her, if thou wilt go with me, then I will go: but if thou wilt not with me, then I will not go (v 8, NIV).*

"And she said, I will surely go with thee notwithstanding the journey that thou takest shall not be for thine honour; for the Lord shall sell Sisera into the hand of a woman. Deborah arose, and went with Barak to Kedeshi" (v 8-9, NIV).

"And the princes of Issachar were with Deborah; along with ten thousands men of Naphtali and Zebulun (4:6, 5:15, NIV).

Prophetess Deborah called upon many great men to help her in leading Israel. Some were honored to assist, while some others refused. She asked Dan and Asher, but they did not help. (Judges 5:16-17 NIV) declares:

"Why abodest thou among the sheepfolks, to hear the bleatings of the flock? For the divisions of Reuben there were great searching of heart.
Gilead abode beyond Jordan: and why did Dan remain in ships. Asher continued on the sea shore, and abode in his breaches.

Deborah sorted the help of Benjamin, Machir and Ephraim. The kings came and fought, the kings of Canaan in Taanach by the waters of Megiddo came and fought. They fought from the heavens; the stars in their courses fought against Sisera" (5:19-20, NIV).

God was clearly in control of this war, He ***"Discomfited Sisera, and with all his chariots, and all his hosts, with the edge of the sword before Barak(15). And, the hand of the children of Israel prospered, and prevailed against Jabin the king of Canaan, until they had destroyed Jabin King of Canaan"*** *(v 24, NIV).* And the land had rest for forty years (v.31, NIV).

In conclusion, God is a deliverer and just as He delivered the children of Israel. He will deliver us when we cry out with a heart of repentance. We have been given the same rights to this freedom through our kinship with Jesus. No trial; nor tribulation shall hold God's children captive in any way, form or shape. For we have been set free through the Blood of Jesus. In our freedom we can say "Yes, Lord! to your will and yes to your way! Yes, Lord Why Not Me?"

Trails will come regardless to one's faith, Christian or no Christian there will be challenges of life. With each blow and with every arduous task, one must not give in to the powers of the enemy. We must fight the good fight, knowing that God is a deliverer.

EPILOGUE

Prior to finishing the final chapters of Lord, Why Me, I could not understand why it was me that had to endure some many trials, tribulation, challenges and changes. However, after concluding this book, I know that I had to face each hurdle in order to grow and mature as an individual and this is why it was me.

With each hardship, it taught me something. I had to learn patience, something I did not have. I had to learn compassion, how to love others regardless to their shortcomings. I finally came to understand that no matter how righteous we would like to be, we will fall in some area of life. As people we are motivated by different things and therefore forgiveness must play a significant role in our daily walk of life. However, in order to forgive those that have trespassed against us, we must know how to love even when we have been done wrong. I have learned how to love others as I love myself.

As I finalized, "Lord! Why Me I was taught the true meaning of obtaining the "Fruit of the Spirit" as according to Galatians 5:22. In doing so, I can write with authority my next book which will be on bookshelves throughout the nation, "**A Prescription for a Shattered Heart.**"

BIBLIOGRAPHY

Holy Bible, New International Bible: Zondervan's Publishing, 1963.

ABOUT THE AUTHOR

Joanna was born to Evans (deceased) and Martha Perdue. She was born in Stuart, Florida on April 3, 1954. During her childhood she lived in Hobe Sound, Florida until the age of twelve. At which time her mother relocated the family to Trenton, New Jersey where she stayed until 1979. When she returned from New Jersey she moved to West Palm Beach, Florida. But now she resides in Orlando, Florida with her three granddaughters.

Her Christian experience consists of the followings: In her earlier years, she was raised as a Baptist, later changing her faith to Pentecostal. However, as she grew spiritually and matured in Christ, she changed her faith to non-denominational.

She is a devout Christian who firmly believes in the Bible in its entirety. She has vowed to win as many souls as she can for the kingdom of God. And it is her desire to tear down the kingdom of the enemy by effectively proclaiming the Gospel of Jesus Christ.

As a result of her desire to win souls for Christ, she has had to endure much spiritual warfare. Spiritual Warfare appeared to be apart of her life from the very onset of conception and has not ceased. However, her faith in God has enabled her to overcome all obstacles.

She has had to climb many rough mountains, walk through steep valleys as she strives to make heaven her home. But through it all, she has held strong to the Word of God.

Her educational background consists of:

An Associate of Science in Dietetic Technology from Palm Beach Community College; located in Lake Worth, Florida. A Bachelor of Health Services from Florida AtlanticUniversity; located in Boca Raton Florida; a Master of Health Management, St. Thomas University; a Master of Ministerial Studies from Truth

Bible College and Seminary and a Doctorate of Theology from the same seminary school; located in Jacksonville, Florida.

Her personal accomplishments esteemed from the help and grace of God. Without God in the midst of her life she could not have successfully accomplished any thing.

She is an ordained minister who operates in the role of an Evangelist/teacher. She is a member of Mt. Olive Missionary Baptist Church located in Hobe Sound, Florida. Her ministry consists of speaking at Women Conferences throughout the United States. She is a member and speakers of "The Heart of a Wounded Woman" founded by Elder Darcel Clemens of Niagara Falls, NY.

Dr. Price is the Chief Executive Officer (CEO) and founder of JD Price Theological Bible College, Inc located in Orlando, Florida. For more information visit (www.jdpricetheologicalbiblecollege.com). She is a part-time Reading Instructor for El Bethel Christian Academy located at 3000 Bruton Boulevard Orlando, Florida where Mrs. Carolyn Thomas is Principal.

She is a licensed Nursing Home Administrator for the State of Florida who performs in an inactive status.

She has been recognized as one of America's 2000 Noticeable Women for her "achievements and outstanding service to community, state and nation."

During the year of 1994/95, she was recognized by "Who's, Who Worldwide" for being an outstanding business leader.

She is a Board of Director member for Our Next Step, Inc.; located in Riviera Beach, Florida, founded by Mr. and Mrs. Renard Matthews.

She is the mother of six children, one deceased (Kesia and grandmother of twenty seven grandchildren.

Her philosophy of life is, "May the work that she does speak for her."

ISBN 141207045-7

Made in the USA
Columbia, SC
28 October 2018